SURVIVING THE DIVINE ASSIGNMENT OF A PASTOR'S WIFE

Navigating Ministry Without Losing Yourself

SALONGE CRENSHAW

Foreword by Pastor Marineka Kenney

Ushindi

Gambrills, MD

Dedication

To every pastor's wife who has ever felt unseen while carrying the unseen weight. May you find peace, purpose, and power in your divine assignment.

CONTENTS

Foreword

In the shadow of the pulpit stands a woman whose strength often goes unnoticed, whose sacrifice is seldom acknowledged, and whose calling is just as sacred, though sometimes less visible, as the one beside whom she stands. Many women hold this position and are all uniquely different, yet we share one thing in common: the commonality of being married to a man who has been called to the ministry of a Pastor. It is a journey filled with both joy and unseen burdens. Yet, few books have dared to reach into this direct space with truth and understanding until now.

The role of a pastor's wife is often complex and quiet, filled with unseen sacrifices, unspoken expectations, and an unwavering need for grace. This is more than just another book. It is a voice of compassion, a source of strength, and a much-needed affirmation for women who find themselves navigating the dual expectations of ministry and marriage, leadership and loneliness, family, and faith. It will speak directly to those who are often expected to have all the answers yet silently wrestle with their own questions.

This book offers practical wisdom, heartfelt encouragement, and spiritual insights drawn from real-life experiences. Whether you are a pastor's wife, a church leader seeking to understand, or a friend who wants to help, this book will illuminate the unique challenges and joys of this often-overlooked calling. This calling is not without its weight. For the woman called to walk beside a pastor—not behind him, not beneath him, but beside him-that weight can feel unbearably heavy.

For the Pastor's wife with those hidden places where weariness meets hope, where service meets solitude, and where faith must be refueled and renewed, this book is for you. Pastor Salonge Crenshaw is stepping into this journey to remind you that you are not alone, through her own experience, knowledge, and wisdom. You will find in the pages of this book godly wisdom and the tools to not just survive in ministry as a pastor's wife but to flourish as an individual.

May this book be a well of encouragement, a source of help, and a reminder that your role matters deeply to your family, your church, and most importantly, to God.

Marineka Kenney
Pastor, Faith Builders Worship Center
And CEO, M&Kompany

Introduction

Why This Book?

Surviving the divine assignment is a guide designed to help you navigate the intricate dance between church obligations, marital harmony, and personal well-being. It is written for you, the pastor's wife who carries the weight of her husband's ministry while striving to nurture her own identity and dreams.

Being a pastor's wife is more than a title—it is a calling. This sacred role places you at the heart of your community's spiritual journey, where you offer support, wisdom, and compassion to others. However, in the process, you must also learn to protect your joy, well-being, and relationships.

The Struggles We Face

Many pastors' wives grapple with the silent burden of unspoken expectations—the pressure to be:

- a spiritual leader in the church,
- a supportive spouse in ministry,
- a loving and present mother,
- and a pillar of the community.

Expecting to excel in every area can lead to stress, self-doubt, and even burnout. This book sheds light on these struggles and offers practical solutions to help you thrive, not just survive, in your divine assignment.

Why I Wrote This Book

I understand these challenges because I have walked this path for over 36 years. My journey as a pastor's wife has been filled with moments of joy, exhaustion, doubt, and growth. Through my experiences, I have learned what works, what does not, and what is necessary for sustaining both ministry and marriage.

Whether you are just beginning this journey or have been living it for years, my goal is to provide the tools, wisdom, and encouragement you need to thrive in your role.

What You Will Gain from This Book

Throughout these pages, you will discover:

- Strategies for achieving balance – so you can serve without sacrificing yourself.
- Stories from other pastors' wives – real experiences, struggles, and victories.
- Practical exercises – to help you reflect, set boundaries, and grow.
- Insights on managing your time – while nurturing your marriage and caring for yourself without compromising your spiritual and communal commitments.

By the end of this book, you will have a roadmap to navigate your divine assignment with grace, wisdom, and resilience.

You are Not Alone!

Take heart, dear sister, you are not alone on this journey. The weight of ministry is real, but so is the strength and grace God provides. You can honor your calling without losing yourself with the right support and strategies.

Let this book be your companion, offering hope, guidance, and the assurance that you can thrive in your divine assignment.

Together, let us uncover the path to serving with joy, loving with strength, and living with balance.

CHAPTER 1
Your Identity

Meet Sally

Sally was newly married and full of excitement as she moved with her husband to a small town where he had been called to pastor a long-established local church. She looked forward to standing beside him in the ministry, eager to embrace this new chapter.

However, she quickly realized just how many expectations came with her role as the pastor's wife. The congregation warmly welcomed them, expressing their delight at having a young pastor and his equally young wife. But soon after, Sally found herself bombarded with advice and opinions on how she should conduct herself.

Some expected her to lead the women's ministry, while others thought she should teach Sunday school. Someone else insisted she take charge of organizing community events. No one asked her what she felt called to do—they assumed she would step into every role presented to her.

In her effort to support her husband and be the "perfect" pastor's wife, Sally stretched herself thin. She tried to meet every demand, hoping to fulfill the congregation's expectations while also keeping her marriage strong. But instead of feeling fulfilled, she became overwhelmed, exhausted, and resentful—not just toward the church, but even toward her husband and the ministry itself.

Doubt crept in. Am I really meant to be a pastor's wife? Can I meet the needs of the congregation without losing myself? Is it possible to serve while still honoring who God created me to be?

Although Sally's name has been changed, her story is all too familiar to many pastors' wives. The tension between external expectations and personal identity is a common struggle.

Throughout this chapter, we will explore how to define, or redefine, yourself beyond the role of "pastor's wife." We will discuss how to embrace the gifts God has uniquely given you, set healthy boundaries, and overcome the doubts that inevitably arise. Being married to a pastor does not mean losing your identity—it means discovering how to serve in a way that aligns with who God has called you to be.

Embracing Your Spiritual Identity: Who Are You in Christ?

Many times, the Pastor's wife never takes the time to embrace her own identity. Either letting it be defined by her family and/or the congregation, with her being the wife and mother first, and whatever is left (if anything) is spent trying to find that small space for herself.

Before anything else, know that you are a child of God, called to live out the purposes He has placed on your life. Even though this is an assignment given by God, it is not the only assignment you have. This means your ultimate identity is not determined by your last name, your husband's position, or the opinions of others. It is anchored in Christ. Understanding this can bring a profound sense of peace and confidence.

Ephesians, chapter one, reminds us we are chosen, loved, and redeemed. Meditating on these truths helps you see yourself through God's eyes, counteracting the pressures to meet everyone else's standards. Daily affirmations in front of the mirror will help you remind yourself of who you are in God.

Make time, notice I did not say, find time. We must make time to truly grasp our identity in Christ by cultivating regular prayer, Bible study, and reflection. Spending quality one-on-one time with God grounds you spiritually and offers clarity when outside voices become overwhelming.

People may refer to you as "the pastor's wife," but remember that this is only one aspect of you. If you only see yourself through this lens, it can overshadow your individuality and limit your personal growth. Instead, consider the role as one channel through which you live out your broader God-given purpose.

Unearthing Your Gifts and Passions

God has given each of us different gifts—teaching, hospitality, administration, creativity, mercy, and more. Your task is to discover and cultivate these gifts, then prayerfully discern how to use them for God's glory.

Sally found herself spending much of her time trying to cultivate gifts that would enhance the ministry of her husband, without trying to discover what her gifts are. Over time, this left her feeling like an impostor, and she soon felt that she was not being true to herself. She was concerned that her gifts, which were entirely different from her husband's, would overshadow his gifts.

You might worry about drawing attention away from your spouse or being perceived too forward. In truth, when you use your gifts, you enhance the church's ministry; your contribution is not competition but a richer expression of God's work. Remember, your gifts are given by God, and they are designed to complement and not compete. Your spouse's pastoral role may include preaching, counseling, or administrative leadership.

Consider how your gifts can complement these responsibilities. If you are strong in communication, you could assist with church newsletters or social media. If you are a gifted listener, you might lead a small group or offer informal mentoring to new members. Communicate openly with your spouse to ensure you feel supported and unified.

Look beyond the church walls. Remember that the ministry is not confined to the church building. Your passions might lead you to volunteer at a local shelter, teach a crafting class, or get involved in community outreach. These initiatives still represent the heart of ministry—loving and serving people in Jesus' name.

Always balance service with self-care. As you step into new areas of ministry, ensure you maintain healthy boundaries. Over-commitment can rob you of the joy these gifts were meant to bring. Schedule time for personal reflection and rest, so you can give from a full rather than a depleted spirit.

Overcoming Self-Doubt and Comparison: The Comparison Trap

Soon after arriving at the church, Sally found herself comparing herself to other women in the ministry in everything from clothes, looks, hair, jobs, and even how she spoke. It was not long before she became very self-conscious about what she would wear to each ministry function. She would spend hours milling over her clothes to put together her most appealing outfit. Sally found herself trying to dress like the other women in church to make herself feel better.

Social media, well-meaning church members, and even your fears can tempt you to compare yourself to other pastors' wives. You might see someone who seems perfect—effortlessly hospitable, an amazing speaker, a flawlessly put-together mother—and wonder, "Why can't I be more like her?"

There are two steps to take whenever you find yourself in this position.

Unrealistic Standards

The first step is to recognize unrealistic standards. Unrealistic standards often arise from a combination of societal ideals, personal insecurities, and the pressure to be exemplary in every aspect of life. As a pastor's wife, you may feel expected to be the perfect host, a spiritual guru, a flawless homemaker, and an ever-patient mother—all at the same time. While it is natural to want to do your best, it is crucial to separate God's true calling for you from the exaggerated expectations placed on you (or that you place on yourself).

It is quite easy to fall into unrealistic standards. Most of them originate from cultural messages, where the "first family" is showcased in a reel of family, faith, and ministry success, often leaving out the struggles and missteps that are part of real life.

These standards can also arise from congregational perceptions. Church members may consciously or unconsciously expect the wife to model "saintly" behavior. It is easy to internalize these expectations, leading one to believe that they must fulfill this role perfectly.

Finally, there is self-imposed pressure. Be careful not to hold yourself to impossible standards out of fear that any weakness will reflect poorly on your husband's ministry. This pressure can certainly lead to burnout, anxiety, or a persistent sense of falling short.

This may sound easy on paper, but I can attest that it is not easy to achieve. You must recognize the red flags in yourself. Some of those red flags are excessive comparison. You may notice yourself frequently saying, "I should be more outgoing like her," or "I wish I could get up and speak like her." This suggests that you are chasing someone else's calling instead of embracing what you bring to the ministry.

Another red flag is feeling guilty or ashamed whenever you say "no." Do not feel guilty about taking time for yourself. If you think that you can attend every function, participate in every service, while neglecting your needs, it is a sure sign that your expectations have become unrealistic. Admit that you cannot be everything to everyone or all things to anyone.

One last red flag is the fear of being authentic. While we do not want to broadcast every issue that arises within your household, do not be afraid to experience a bad minute, hour, day, or month.

Unrealistic standards hurt. They cause emotional strain. The constant push to measure up can lead to anxiety and self-doubt. They can cause spiritual fatigue – when you believe your worth is tied to your performance, it is easy to lose sight of God's grace. You find yourself feeling disconnected, even resentful about your ministry involvement. It can have a major impact on relationships with you and the members of the church, especially the ones who can sense your authenticity, because it will show.

These unrealistic standards can cause problems between you and your spouse if you are constantly stressed. Remember, these standards are unrealistic, and if you want your husband to make you feel better about not meeting them, and he is perplexed, this feeling can lead to loneliness and resentment towards his relationship with the congregation.

There are ways to manage these unrealistic standards, but you must do the hard work. Name the unrealistic standard and reframe the narrative. The moment you catch yourself thinking "I should be able to do it all," pause. Ask, "Is this truly God's expectation of me—or a reflection of someone else's demands?" Then replace that lie with a biblical truth, such as Psalm 139:14, *"I will praise thee; for I am fearfully and wonderfully made: marvelous are thy works; and that my soul knoweth right well."* This scripture affirms your God-given uniqueness.

Applaud yourself. Instead of waiting to applaud yourself only when you have checked every imaginary box, celebrate the small victories—a thoughtful conversation with a church member, a meaningful moment of prayer, or a simple act of self-care.

Set manageable goals. Determine what you realistically have time and energy for, then establish boundaries around everything else. If you feel called to host a women's Bible study, for instance, plan it in a way that will not compromise your own health or family time.

Seek out an accountability partner. Share your struggles with a trusted mentor or counselor. They can help you recognize when you are slipping into perfectionistic patterns and remind you of God's grace. The worst thing you can do is to be your own counselor – others sometimes can recognize what you do not want to admit to. Allow yourself to be held accountable.

Ultimately, recognizing unrealistic standards is about remembering who you are in Christ. God did not call you to be flawless; He called you to be faithful. By adjusting your perspective, you can let go of the compulsion to please everyone and instead focus on living authentically in your divine assignment. When you release yourself from impossible ideals, you open the door to genuine growth, deeper relationships, and renewed joy in both your personal life and your ministry.

Expanding your awareness of these unrealistic standards is the first step toward a more balanced, grace-filled approach to your role as a pastor's wife. Embracing realistic goals and biblical truth will enable you to serve wholeheartedly without sacrificing your well-being or sense of self in the process.

Remember to stay grounded in gratitude; God could have given this assignment to any other woman, but He gave it to you. Spending time focusing on what you do have and what you can do shifts your perspective away from scarcity or inadequacy.

Facing Insecurities

The second step is to face insecurities head-on. Sally faced many insecurities when she started working in the ministry with her husband. She dealt with the fact that he was the one they wanted; she just came along because she was married to him. She had never worked much in any ministry growing up. She had attended church most of her life, but never to the extent of what her husband had, nor had she achieved any of the recognition that he had. So, she knew that he was a sought-after pastor, but what about her? There were so many times she felt unheard by him and the congregation, which made her feel inadequate and sometimes out of place.

Insecurities often creep in when you least expect them, sometimes through a single critical comment from a church member, a social media post showcasing someone else's seemingly perfect life, or even your internal dialogue questioning your competence. While insecurities are common and can arise for various reasons, they do not have to dictate how you serve or how you perceive yourself. Confronting these fears and doubts directly can empower you to live and minister with confidence, authenticity, and grace.

Honestly identifying the root of our insecurities. What are your triggers? What are the situations that seem to send you into a tailspin? Is it when you are expected to speak publicly, manage a large event, or counsel someone? Be honest with yourself – ask yourself why you feel insecure in this area. Is it the fear of failure, disappointing your husband, the congregation, or one of those unrealistic expectations? When you pinpoint the core belief, this will allow you to confront it with the truth.

Counter negative thoughts with truth, the Word of God. Use it as a weapon against insecurities. When plagued with self-doubt that says you are inadequate, remind yourself of 2 Corinthians 12:9: *"My grace is sufficient for you, for my power is made perfect in weakness."*

Affirm your call. Remember that God called you into this assignment. The Word tells us in Hebrews 13:21, *"...God will equip us with all we need to do His will and the works that will please Him."* God has equipped you to do the work He has placed in your hands. Remember, you are wonderfully made, and this work is uniquely designed for you. There are times when you must revisit those truths in your life to anchor you when insecurity tries to throw you off.

Practice self-care or self-compassion. Be careful not to slip into the mindset that the pastor's wife must be superhuman. Allow yourself grace—to have off days, to say "I don't know" or "I have never spoken before a group before, let me get my nerves together," or something simple like "can I get some help?" This does not make you less than; it is always wise to be honest. If we do not want to be perceived as a superwoman, then we do not want to perpetuate the problem by giving the false impression of that very thing.

Do not spend too much time on what you could not do; celebrate those helped by what you did. Do not dwell on your mistakes, those who did not respond positively, or those who chose not to show up. Instead, celebrate that what God called you to do has been accomplished – that God is pleased.

Embracing your identity in Christ, discovering your distinct gifts, and stepping into your calling with confidence will set the tone for how you approach every other aspect of ministry life. Keep in mind: the God who called you is faithful, and He equips you to be exactly who He has created you to be—even in the spotlight of pastoral ministry.

Reflection Questions

1. In what ways have I allowed the title "pastor's wife" to overshadow my personal identity?

2. Which Bible verses or passages most strongly remind me of my worth in Christ?

3. What gifts or passions excite me to explore or develop further?

4. When do I typically experience self-doubt, and what truth can I lean on to counter those thoughts?

5. Who can I invite into my journey—friends, mentors, or fellow pastors' wives—to offer wisdom and accountability?

6. What unrealistic expectations—whether self-imposed or imposed by others—do I need to release to walk freely in my God-given purpose?

7. How can I cultivate self-compassion when I fall short, and what does grace look like in this stage of my life?

Journal Your Thoughts

CHAPTER 2
The Divine Assignment

Meet Camilla

When Camilla married her pastor husband, he had already been leading the church for many years and was well-respected in the community. She was excited to become the wife of a man of God, believing that his love for God would naturally extend to her, cherishing and honoring her as the scriptures taught. She eagerly anticipated working alongside him in ministry while also fulfilling the role of the devoted wife he said he needed and wanted.

However, reality quickly set in, and Camilla realized that marriage to a pastor was far different from what she had imagined. She understood her husband was dedicated to the ministry and his congregation, but she was unprepared for the sacrifices it would demand from their marriage. She had not anticipated the constant interruptions—the last-minute changes in plans, the late-night emergency calls, or the long hours after church when he stayed behind for counseling sessions, leaving her waiting in the background. No one seemed to consider how she felt, and when she expressed her frustrations, he defended his responsibilities rather than acknowledging her concerns.

Despite her genuine love for people and her active involvement in the church—building relationships with members and volunteering at outreach events—she often felt overlooked and sidelined by the very man she had married. Over time, resentment began to creep in. She struggled with the expectations placed on them both and felt as though the congregation demanded more of her husband's time and attention than she did.

She understood that ministering to others was part of his calling, but no one had ever explained what was expected of her. Where did she fit in? What was her role in this divine assignment?

The role of a pastor's wife is often described as a calling rather than merely a supportive position in the church. It is a unique and demanding assignment that requires grace, wisdom, and a deep sense of purpose. It involves navigating complex responsibilities while maintaining faith, identity, and a healthy marriage amidst unspoken expectations.

Understanding the Divine Nature of the Role

Being a pastor's wife is more than just a position; it is a calling that God entrusts to you. This assignment carries a divine purpose, as you are positioned to influence not only your family but also the wider church community. Recognizing the divine nature of this role helps you embrace the responsibilities with a sense of mission and dedication.

Spiritual support. You are called to be a spiritual support for your husband and a beacon of faith within the church. This role requires you to lean on God for strength, wisdom, and guidance as you navigate the complexities of ministry life.

Modeling Christlike behavior. The divine assignment involves modeling Christlike behavior in your interactions and offering grace, compassion, and love to those around you. Your life serves as a living testimony of God's work and presence.

Balancing multiple roles within the assignment. The divine assignment involves balancing multiple roles, each with its own set of expectations and challenges. Understanding these roles helps in managing them effectively without feeling overwhelmed.

Wife and partner. As a wife, your primary role is to support your husband in his pastoral duties while nurturing your marriage. This requires maintaining open communication, offering emotional support, and being a partner in prayer and decision-making.

Mother and caregiver. If you have children, the divine assignment extends to being a nurturing and guiding presence in their lives, balancing their needs with the demands of the church.

Church leader and mentor. Within the church, you may be called to lead women's ministries, mentor younger women, or organize church events. This leadership role requires a blend of humility and authority, as you serve and guide others.

Community influencer. Outside the church, you may find opportunities to influence the broader community through outreach programs, charity work, or simply by being a positive presence in your neighborhood.

As you can see from the above-mentioned list, the roles of a pastor's wife resemble those of a trapeze artist. While the divine assignment is a noble calling, it also presents its own set of challenges that require perseverance and faith. This section will outline some of these challenges and how to overcome them.

Public scrutiny. As a pastor's wife, you often find yourself in the public eye, subject to scrutiny and criticism from both the congregation and the community. This situation is not necessarily the congregation's fault, but rather the result of ingrained expectations—beliefs that have been unconsciously programmed into the minds of the people.

In Camilla's case, her husband had been leading the church long before she married him. The congregation, having cared for and supported him for years, felt a sense of responsibility in ensuring that he chose the "right" woman to stand beside him in ministry. Before she entered the picture, they had looked out for him, which led to a strong sense of ownership over his well-being. To them, he was their pastor first.

As a result, Camilla found herself under constant scrutiny. Every aspect of her life was observed: what she wore, how she spoke, her level of church involvement, and even how her husband appeared in public. The congregation, whether consciously or not, placed the weight of his well-being on her shoulders. This unspoken pressure created a strain not only on Camilla but also on her relationship with the church community, making it difficult for her to find her footing in her new role.

The Weight of Expectations

The role of a pastor's wife often comes with a long list of unwritten expectations. From being the perfect hostess at church events to offering a listening ear to every member of the congregation, the weight of these responsibilities can feel overwhelming. These expectations are not just imposed by others—they are also self-inflicted, as many pastors' wives hold themselves to impossibly high standards, striving to meet every need and fulfill every role.

It is important to recognize the danger of trying to meet every expectation placed upon us. It is an easy trap to fall into, often without realizing the toll it takes—emotionally, mentally, and spiritually.

Congregations often see the pastor's wife as a secondary leader, expecting her to be involved in everything from choir rehearsals to counseling sessions. This perception can blur the boundaries between personal life and ministry, making it difficult to carve out time for rest and personal well-being. Imagine living in a constant spotlight, where every action is scrutinized, and every word is weighed. It is a challenge that many pastors' wives understand all too well.

These expectations carry an invisible burden—one that is not always recognized at first. Over time, however, pressure builds, leading to exhaustion, stress, and, in some cases, even resentment. A pastor's wife must learn to set healthy boundaries, embrace grace, and remember that her primary calling is not to meet every demand, but to walk in alignment with God's purpose for her life.

These expectations are associated with stress levels that are not initially recognized.

Internal expectations. Internal expectations are the self-imposed standards and pressures that many pastors' wives carry. These arise from a combination of personal beliefs, a sense of duty, and a deep desire to meet the spiritual, emotional, and practical needs of both their families and church communities. While some of these expectations can be motivating and lead to personal growth, others can become overwhelming and even harmful if not kept in balance.

Recognizing and managing these internal pressures is crucial. Without proper boundaries, the weight of trying to live up to an idealized version of the pastor's wife can lead to exhaustion, self-doubt, and an unhealthy sense of responsibility. It is important to remember that true success in this role does not come from perfection but from walking in grace, embracing one's unique calling, and trusting God to fill the gaps where human effort falls short.

Pressure to be a perfect role model. One of the most common internal expectations faced by pastors' wives is the pressure to be a flawless role model for the congregation. Many feel they must embody the ideal Christian woman: strong in faith, wise in counsel, and unwavering in character. However, this expectation can be exhausting, leaving little room for personal struggles, growth, or even the grace to be human.

This pressure often stems from the belief that their actions are under constant scrutiny and that any perceived misstep could reflect poorly on their husband's ministry. As a result, many pastors' wives fall into a cycle of self-monitoring—carefully weighing every word and action for fear of judgment. Over time, this can lead to anxiety, self-doubt, and a deep-seated fear of failure.

Yet, true leadership is not about perfection; it is about authenticity. A pastor's wife does not need to be without flaws to be an effective example of faith. Instead, embracing vulnerability, seeking support, and allowing God's grace to work through imperfections can be the most powerful testimony of all.

Balancing public and private personas, the dual role of being a public figure within the church and a private individual at home creates a complex dynamic. Pastors' wives may feel compelled to present a polished and composed persona in public, regardless of their private struggles or challenges. This internal expectation to switch between these roles seamlessly can be mentally and emotionally taxing.

Maintaining this balance often leads to a suppression of personal needs and emotions, as individuals prioritize the church's perception over their well-being. Over time, this can foster feelings of isolation, preventing them from sharing their true selves with others, including their congregation and sometimes even their spouse.

The expectation of spiritual perfection. Many pastors' wives feel an internal pressure to display an unwavering spiritual life, characterized by constant growth, deep faith, and a visible prayer life. They might believe they should have answers to every spiritual question and provide unwavering support to others, even when they themselves are struggling with doubt, fatigue, or spiritual dryness.

This expectation can lead to feelings of guilt or inadequacy when individuals experience natural ebbs in their spiritual journey. The fear of being perceived as spiritually weak may prevent them from seeking help or admitting their struggles, which can further isolate them.

For example, Camilla had a fondness for dramatic soap operas. She knew these shows were purely fictional, often centered around adultery, deception, and the more scandalous aspects of life; yet, she enjoyed the storytelling and the drama. However, she soon found herself feeling embarrassed about her interest in them, especially at the thought of anyone in the congregation discovering her guilty pleasure.

The weight of expectation pressed down on her. Was it appropriate for a pastor's wife to watch such shows? Would people judge her for it? The guilt became so overwhelming that she eventually decided to stop watching altogether, convincing herself that it was not fitting for someone in her position.

The need to please everyone. The internal drive to be everything to everyone is a common struggle for many pastors' wives. They often take on multiple roles—counselor, mentor, event organizer, and ministry leader—while striving to meet the expectations of both their congregation and their family. The desire to please everyone can quickly become an overwhelming burden as they attempt to juggle countless responsibilities without letting anyone down.

This relentless need to satisfy others often leads to overcommitment, leaving little time for personal rest or family life. It creates an unsustainable cycle of constantly pouring into others while neglecting one's own well-being. Over time, this can take a toll—physically, emotionally, and spiritually—resulting in exhaustion, resentment, and even burnout.

Breaking free from this cycle requires setting healthy boundaries and understanding that true ministry is not about meeting every demand but about serving with wisdom and balance. A pastor's wife must remember that she is not called to carry every burden alone—her well-being matters, too.

Managing Expectations

Managing expectations involves a conscious effort to redefine what success and fulfillment mean in the context of being a pastor's wife. Here are some strategies to help manage these pressures:

Self-compassion. Give yourself some grace. Practice self-compassion by acknowledging that it is okay to have limits and imperfections. This does not mean your issues should be put on display for public scrutiny or examination, but do not feel guilty for having a bad minute, hour, day, or month. Understand that being human sometimes means falling short, which is perfectly acceptable.

Realistic standards. Set realistic and achievable standards for yourself. Recognize that you cannot do everything, and prioritize what is most important for your well-being and that of your family. Understand that you cannot be everything to everyone and all things to anyone.

Seek support. Engage with trusted friends, mentors, or support groups who understand the unique challenges of ministry life. The keyword in this statement is 'trusted.' Unfortunately, your circle of friends should remain small. Learn to recognize true support rather than someone who merely desires to be in your space. Sharing your experiences and receiving encouragement can help alleviate the weight of internal expectations.

Regular reflection. Set aside time to reflect regularly on your internal expectations and evaluate whether they are healthy and realistic. Adjust your expectations as needed to ensure they align with your values and capabilities.

Professional help. Do not hesitate to seek professional counseling or coaching if internal pressures become overwhelming. There is no harm in seeking professional counseling. We were always taught that saved individuals did not seek secular counseling. It is always better to get unbiased advice. A counselor can provide strategies to manage stress and build resilience.

By recognizing and addressing these internal expectations, pastors' wives can foster a healthier self-view, allowing them to serve their families and congregations more authentically and sustainably

Embracing the assignment with grace. Embracing the divine assignment of being a pastor's wife means accepting both its challenges and blessings with grace, faith, and resilience. It requires acknowledging that this role is not about achieving perfection, but about walking in obedience to God's calling, leaning on His strength, and trusting His plan—even when the journey feels overwhelming.

Shifting perspective. One of the first steps in embracing this role is understanding that the expectations placed on a pastor's wife, whether external or internal, should never overshadow her personal relationship with God. It is easy to fall into the trap of performing for others, striving to meet their demands while neglecting her own spiritual and emotional needs. However, true fulfillment comes when she prioritizes God's expectations over people's, allowing His grace to sustain her through every season of ministry.

Finding strength in God's grace is essential. Grace is not only essential for others but also for oneself. A pastor's wife must give herself permission to grow, to make mistakes, and to rely on God's sufficiency rather than her efforts. There will be days of exhaustion, discouragement, and self-doubt, but God's grace is always enough. Instead of striving for perfection, she must embrace the reality that God's power is made perfect in weakness (2 Corinthians 12:9).

Setting healthy boundaries. Another important aspect of embracing this assignment is learning to establish healthy boundaries. This topic will be discussed more thoroughly in the next chapter. It is easy for a pastor's wife to feel obligated to say "yes" to every request, leading ministries, counseling, attending every event, and always being available. While serving is an essential part of ministry, it should never come at the cost of personal well-being or family relationships. Saying "no" when necessary does not mean failing in ministry; it means recognizing that she cannot pour into others if she is spiritually, emotionally, and physically depleted.

Walking in authenticity. One of the greatest gifts a pastor's wife can offer is her authenticity. She does not have to pretend to be perfect, always strong, or without struggles. Her transparency in sharing her faith journey, including the hardships, can inspire and encourage those around her. People connect with realness, and by being open about her growth, struggles, and victories, she becomes a powerful testament to God's grace at work.

Embracing the assignment with confidence. Ultimately, embracing the divine assignment is about trusting God's plan and stepping into the role with confidence, not fear. It involves recognizing that she was chosen for this path, not because she is perfect, but because God has equipped her for the journey. A pastor's wife can serve with joy, resilience, and unwavering faith by surrendering the pressures of people-pleasing, letting go of unrealistic expectations, and standing firm in her identity in Christ.

Rather than simply enduring challenges, she can embrace them, knowing that God's grace is sufficient, His strength is endless, and His purpose for her life is greater than any expectations the world could ever place upon her.

Finding Joy and Fulfillment in the Assignment

Despite the challenges, the divine assignment of being a pastor's wife is also filled with moments of joy, fulfillment, and purpose. Embracing these moments allows you to see the beauty and impact of your role, reminding you that this calling is not just about sacrifice but also about the incredible blessings that come with it.

Celebrating successes. Take time to acknowledge and celebrate both the big and small victories in your ministry and personal life. Whether it is a successful church event, a meaningful conversation that encouraged someone, or a moment of spiritual breakthrough, recognize the positive impact you have on your church and community. These milestones remind us of God's faithfulness and the value of your role.

Witnessing growth. One of the greatest rewards of this divine assignment is witnessing the spiritual transformation of those you serve. Seeing church members grow in their faith, families restored, and individuals finding purpose in God is a powerful testament to the work you and your husband are doing. Knowing that you have played a part in someone's journey toward Christ brings deep satisfaction and a renewed sense of mission.

Personal growth. The challenges of this role often lead to personal and spiritual growth. While the pressures can be demanding, they also shape you into a stronger, more compassionate, and more resilient individual. You learn patience through trials, wisdom through experience, and faith through dependence on God. Each challenge you face refines you, deepening your understanding of grace and strengthening your ability to lead and support others.

Finding joy and fulfillment in this assignment is about shifting your focus, choosing to see the blessings rather than just the burdens. It is about embracing moments of laughter, gratitude, and spiritual breakthroughs. And most importantly, it is remembering that your calling is not only serving others but also allowing God to work in and through you, shaping you for His greater purpose.

Reflection Questions

1. How does viewing your role as a divine assignment change the way you approach its challenges and responsibilities?

2. In what ways can a pastor's wife serve as spiritual support to her husband and the church?

3. What does it mean to model Christlike behavior in daily interactions?

4. What strategies can a pastor's wife use to balance her roles as a wife, mother, church leader, and community influencer?

5. Why is open communication in marriage essential for maintaining a healthy ministry partnership?

6. How can a pastor's wife ensure that she prioritizes her family's needs while fulfilling her ministry duties?

7. Why do public scrutiny and congregational expectations create added pressure for a pastor's wife?

CHAPTER 3
Balancing Marriage and Ministry

Meet Taneka

Taneka and her Pastor husband have been married for 10 years. In those 10 years, they had three children under the age of 10 and both worked full-time jobs. While they worked diligently in the ministry, their three children were active in extra-curricular activities – dance class and Little League sports. Taneka would find her days filled with work obligations, then come home after a long day to become a free Uber, taking her children to all their activities, and still manage to attend all the church activities.

Taneka finds herself tired and overwhelmed at the end of each day. On the other hand, while she was busy taking care of her responsibilities, her husband was consumed with church responsibilities. She realized after 10 years that she was losing the intimate connection with her husband. She realized they no longer talked, except to sync their schedules, and that her entire life revolved around her career, her children, and the church.

When you and your spouse both serve in ministry—especially as a pastor and pastor's wife—your relationship can quickly become overshadowed by church obligations. Meetings, counseling sessions, community outreach, and even social events can crowd the calendar, making it difficult to spend quality time together as a couple. Yet a healthy marriage not only nourishes you personally but also strengthens your collective witness. This chapter offers strategies to help you preserve and enrich your marital bond while navigating the complexities of church life.

The Dual Commitment: Strategies for Balancing Marriage and Ministry:

Marriage is a sacred covenant—a promise to love, cherish, and support one another through every season of life. For a pastor's wife, this covenant extends into the realm of ministry, creating a unique dynamic where personal and spiritual commitments intertwine. This dual commitment is a delicate balancing act, requiring a harmonious blend of nurturing the marriage and fulfilling ministry obligations.

As a pastor's wife, you are often seen as an extension of your husband's ministry, a partner not only in life but also in service to the church. This role can be both rewarding and overwhelming. The church community may look to you for leadership, support, and involvement in various activities. You might find yourself wearing multiple hats - organizing events, offering counsel, or simply being a visible figure of encouragement. These expectations, while fulfilling, can sometimes overshadow the primary commitment to your marriage.

One of the challenges of this dual commitment is the constant demand for time and attention from both the church and your spouse. Ministry work can be all-consuming, with your husband frequently engaged in meetings, sermons, pastoral care, and community outreach. The church's needs often extend into evenings, weekends, and even holidays, leaving little time for you to nurture your relationship as a couple. This can lead to feelings of neglect or imbalance, where the marriage may seem to take a backseat to the ministry.

Moreover, the emotional toll of ministry can be significant. Both you and your husband may encounter stress, criticism, and the burden of caring for the spiritual well-being of others. Without intentional efforts to support one another, this pressure can strain your marriage, creating a sense of isolation or burnout.

However, it is important to understand that a thriving marriage is not only beneficial but essential to the success of your ministry. A healthy, loving relationship serves as a strong foundation from which you can both draw strength and stability. Your marriage can be a testament to the congregation, showing how love and commitment can withstand the pressures of life and ministry.

To balance these dual commitments effectively, intentionality is key. It requires setting priorities, establishing boundaries, and making deliberate choices to protect your marital bond. This may mean scheduling regular date nights, maintaining open lines of communication, and ensuring that your marriage remains a sanctuary where both partners feel valued and supported.

In the following sections, we will delve deeper into strategies for nurturing your marriage amidst the demands of ministry. We will explore practical ways to communicate, prioritize quality time, and create a partnership that not only survives but thrives within the context of your divine assignment.

Prioritize Your Marriage

In the life of a pastor's wife, the demands of ministry can often overshadow personal relationships, especially the marriage. However, a strong and healthy marriage is not only foundational for personal well-being but also for effective ministry. Prioritizing your marriage amidst the responsibilities of ministry requires intentional effort and conscious decisions to ensure that your relationship remains nurtured and resilient.

Schedule regular time together. Time is one of the most valuable resources in a marriage, especially in a demanding environment. Regularly scheduled time for just the two of you helps maintain connection and intimacy.

Date nights. Make date nights a regular occurrence. Whether it is a dinner out, a movie at home, or a walk in the park, these moments help you reconnect and keep the romance alive. Even simple, low-cost activities can strengthen your bond.

Daily check-ins. Even on busy days, take a few moments to check in with each other. Ask about each other's day, share highlights, and express support. These small conversations can make a significant difference in maintaining a sense of partnership.

Vacation and retreats. Plan for periodic getaways, even if it is just a weekend retreat. Time away from the usual environment allows you to focus on each other without the distractions of ministry and everyday responsibilities. Never cancel a planned vacation or retreat for a church event.

Create a no-ministry zone. Establishing boundaries between ministry and personal life is essential for maintaining a healthy marriage. A no-ministry zone provides intentional time and space where church responsibilities are set aside, allowing you to focus solely on your relationship.

Evening or weekend cut-off. Many church members assume their pastor is available 24/7, but even pastors need time to rest and recharge. Set a firm evening or weekend cut-off time for ministry discussions, except in cases of extreme emergencies. Choose a specific time each day or designated days each week when ministry topics are off-limits. Use this time to engage in activities you both enjoy—whether it is watching a movie, taking a walk, or simply having an uninterrupted conversation. Protecting this time helps reinforce your connection outside of the ministry.

Sacred spaces. Designate a physical space in your home as ministry-free, starting with your bedroom. The marriage bed is sacred and should always remain a place of intimacy, rest, and connection, free from the pressures of ministry. There should be no exceptions to this boundary. Additionally, your bedroom should be off-limits to visitors, reinforcing its role as a private retreat for you and your spouse. Creating this sacred space strengthens your emotional and physical bond, ensuring that your relationship remains a priority.

By setting these boundaries, you cultivate a marriage that is not solely defined by ministry but is nurtured by love, intentional time, and sacred spaces dedicated to just the two of you.

Celebrating milestones. Celebrating milestones and achievements in your marriage reinforces the importance of your relationship. It serves as a reminder to appreciate and acknowledge each other's presence, contributions, and growth, both within and beyond the ministry.

Anniversaries and birthdays. These special days should always remain sacred, no matter how busy the ministry gets. Ministry obligations will always exist, but your relationship deserves intentional celebration. It does not have to be extravagant; what matters most is the thoughtfulness behind the gesture. Whether it is a quiet dinner, a heartfelt letter, or a simple getaway, taking time to honor these moments strengthens your bond and reaffirms your commitment to each other.

Outside successes. Ministry is a big part of your lives, but it is not the only aspect that defines you. Celebrate each other's personal achievements—whether it is earning a degree, landing a job promotion, or reaching a personal goal. Recognizing and honoring your spouse's hard work fosters mutual respect and admiration, reminding both of you that you are whole individuals with dreams and aspirations beyond the church.

Taking the time to celebrate each other not only nurtures your marriage but also sets an example for those you lead, showing that a strong, thriving relationship is built on love, appreciation, and intentionality.

Support each other's roles. Being each other's strongest supporter is essential in marriage, especially when both partners are involved in ministry. A united front not only strengthens your relationship but also sets a powerful example for those you serve.

Be present. Attend each other's significant ministry events whenever possible. Your presence demonstrates solidarity and sends a message to the congregation that you stand together in your calling. In some smaller churches, where the pastor is often the final authority on leadership roles, a simple nod, smile, or "Amen" from your husband can solidify your leadership in the eyes of the congregation. Unfortunately, some members may hesitate to accept your role until they see his visible approval. Standing together helps establish your position while reinforcing a culture of mutual respect.

Encouragement and affirmation. Regularly offer words of encouragement. Ministry can be exhausting, and having a spouse who affirms your efforts makes a significant difference. Recognize and celebrate each other's contributions, reminding one another of the impact you are making. A simple, heartfelt acknowledgment can boost confidence and morale.

Shared responsibilities. Understand each other's roles and, whenever possible, share the load. Ministry should not create division but rather serve as a shared mission where both partners feel equally valued and supported. By collaborating and respecting each other's strengths, you cultivate a balanced, unified partnership that enhances both your marriage and your ministry.

Navigate Conflicts Constructively

Conflicts are inevitable in any relationship, but how you manage them can determine the health and strength of your marriage. In ministry, unresolved conflicts can not only damage your relationship but also have a lasting impact on the congregation. It is crucial that disagreements remain private and that church members are never involved in resolving personal conflicts. However, tensions can sometimes arise due to church members, adding another layer of complexity.

At the beginning of this chapter, we meet Taneka. One afternoon after service, she had a misunderstanding with a parishioner that left her feeling deeply disrespected.

Frustrated, she entered her husband's office, seeking support and validation. Instead of listening to her concerns, he immediately defended the church member. What started as an attempt to express her feelings quickly escalated into a heated conflict. Overcome with anger, Taneka stormed out of the office, right past congregants waiting to speak with her husband, and left the church entirely, while her pastor-husband remained behind, alone in his office.

While this may seem extreme, situations like this occur more often than many realize. They stem from one party feeling unheard and the other feeling torn between their roles. Many pastors find themselves in a constant tug-of-war between their congregation, who depend on them for spiritual guidance, and their wives and families, who are expected to "always" have access to them. The unspoken assumption is that while the congregation needs the pastor, his family should instinctively understand and accept his divided attention.

To maintain a healthy marriage and ministry, it is crucial to navigate conflicts with wisdom and purpose. Below are key strategies for addressing disagreements constructively, ensuring that both your relationship and your ministry remain strong.

Open communication. In marriage, especially in ministry, you must be each other's safe space. It is easy to avoid difficult conversations to maintain peace, telling yourself you do not want to "rock the boat," or convincing yourself that an issue is not that big of a deal. However, ignoring problems does not make them disappear; it only allows resentment to build over time.

Address concerns as they arise rather than allowing them to fester. Approach each discussion with honesty and kindness. Your goal is not to win an argument but to strengthen your relationship. Instead of placing blame, focus on understanding one another's perspectives and working towards a solution together. Healthy and open communication is the foundation of a strong marriage and a thriving ministry.

Prioritize intentional conversations: Set aside dedicated time for regular discussions where you can openly share your feelings, challenges, and successes—both in marriage and in ministry. These intentional check-ins help keep both partners informed, connected, and aligned in their journey together.

Be honest about your needs. Too often, we hesitate to express our concerns out of fear of burdening our spouse. However, true partnership thrives on transparency. Openly communicating your emotions and expectations fosters a deeper understanding, allowing both partners to provide the necessary support. A marriage rooted in honesty and mutual care not only strengthens your relationship but also establishes a solid foundation for an effective ministry.

Use a code word for clarity and boundaries. Develop a code word or phrase that signals when you need to discuss something important or step away from ministry pressures. This simple yet effective tool helps create a moment of pause, allowing both of you to recognize when a serious conversation is needed without adding immediate stress or tension.

A code word can also serve as a gentle way to indicate when one of you feels overwhelmed and needs a break, whether from a heated discussion, an exhausting church situation, or ministry demands. This approach fosters sensitivity and ensures that difficult moments are navigated with mutual respect and understanding. By implementing this strategy, you create a healthy communication buffer that prioritizes both emotional well-being and relational harmony.

Seek resolution, not victory. Open communication is essential, but it is only the first step—conflicts still need resolution. When disagreements arise, approach them with the goal of finding a solution rather than proving a point or "winning" the argument. A healthy marriage, especially in the ministry, thrives on teamwork, not competition.

Compromise and mutual understanding should be the priority. Listen with an open heart, acknowledge each other's feelings, and work toward a resolution that honors both perspectives. Resolving conflicts with love and humility not only strengthens your marriage but also sets a powerful example of grace and unity for those you serve in ministry.

Seek counseling. Do not hesitate to seek guidance from trusted counselors or mentors when conflicts become difficult to navigate on your own. Ministry can be isolating, and the pressures of balancing marriage and leadership can sometimes feel overwhelming. An outside perspective, whether from a professional counselor, a seasoned pastoral couple, or a mentor, can provide valuable insights, objective guidance, and practical strategies for resolution.

Seeking help is not a sign of weakness; it demonstrates wisdom and a commitment to a healthy marriage. Just as you invest in others, allow yourself to be invested in. Prioritizing your relationship through counseling or mentorship not only strengthens your marriage but also ensures that you serve from a place of wholeness.

Pray Together

Prayer is one of the most powerful tools for nurturing a strong, faith-filled marriage, especially when navigating the unique challenges of ministry. It deepens spiritual intimacy, fosters unity, and serves as a constant reminder that God is at the center of your relationship.

Daily prayer. Establish a routine of praying together each day. Whether it is a brief prayer in the morning, before meals, or at bedtime, these moments create a spiritual connection that strengthens your bond. Consistency in prayer reinforces your shared commitment to God and to each other.

Pray for each other. Make it a habit to lift your spouse in prayer, interceding for their needs, concerns, and ministry. Knowing that your partner supports you in prayer offers comfort, encouragement, and spiritual strength. It also cultivates a deeper sense of support, ensuring that you both feel seen, valued, and uplifted.

Prioritizing prayer in your marriage not only fortifies your relationship but also equips you to serve effectively in ministry, united, strengthened, and guided by God's wisdom.

Establish Healthy Boundaries

Establishing healthy boundaries is essential for maintaining balance and well-being in the life of a pastor's wife. Boundaries serve as limits that protect your time, energy, and emotional health while allowing you to fulfill your roles in both marriage and ministry effectively. Without clear boundaries, it is easy to become overwhelmed by the demands of the church, community, and personal life. This section explores how to identify, set, and maintain these crucial boundaries.

Boundaries are not to create barriers or distance yourself from others, but to set clear limits to protect your well-being. They help define what you are willing to do and what you need to reserve for your personal life. Without boundaries, it is easy to overcommit, leading to burnout, resentment, and a strained marriage.

Healthy boundaries ensure that you have time for yourself and your family, separate from your ministry duties. They enable you to serve others effectively without sacrificing your own needs and relationships.

Identify areas that need boundaries. To establish healthy boundaries, evaluate different areas of your life where boundaries may be lacking. Consider the following areas:

Time. How much time do you spend on church-related activities versus personal or family time? Is there a clear distinction between your ministry hours and personal hours?

Reflecting on how I allocated my time between church-related activities and personal life, I realized that when my sons were younger, I was more intentional about prioritizing family. I made it a point to attend their sports practices and games—not for my enjoyment, but for their sake. However, even when I was not physically engaged in church activities, my mind remained preoccupied with them.

I structured my schedule around church commitments, ensuring that my children's events did not conflict with ministry responsibilities, rather than considering whether church activities interfered with my family life. Over time, I recognized that I had failed to establish clear boundaries. I had unconsciously become an extension of my husband's ministry, and my children had become an extension of me, rather than individuals with their own needs and priorities. This realization made me rethink how I balanced my roles as a pastor's wife, a mother, and a person with my own identity.

Responsibilities. Are you taking on more church responsibilities than you can handle? Do you feel obligated to say yes to every request?

One of the core responsibilities of ministry is to empower others—to guide and encourage them in their walk with Christ. However, in our dedication to serving, it is easy to become so consumed with church duties that we lose sight of our own lives outside of the ministry.

We must be mindful not to create unrealistic expectations, whether for ourselves or others, by attempting to attend every church-related event. Participating in every function, from birthday parties to weddings and baby showers, is neither our role nor our obligation. Leadership does not mean sacrificing personal balance to meet every expectation placed upon us.

Remember, your calling is to serve God, not just to live for the people of the church. Setting healthy boundaries is essential for longevity in ministry and personal well-being.

Emotional energy. Do you often feel emotionally drained after interacting with church members? Can you separate their issues from your personal emotional well-being?

It is easy to become emotionally entangled in the struggles of those we serve—we love them, we want them to thrive, and we deeply desire for them to experience the fullness of God's blessings. However, they must also desire these things for themselves.

As leaders, we must be cautious not to take on the burdens of others to the extent that we lose ourselves in their struggles. While compassion is essential, there is a fine line between supporting others and carrying their weight as our own. If we become too emotionally involved, it can cloud our ability to lead with wisdom and objectivity.

Prioritizing our personal well-being is not selfish; it is necessary. To effectively serve, we must ensure that we are spiritually, emotionally, and mentally whole. Only then can we pour into others without depleting ourselves.

Physical space. Do you have a space at home free from ministry work, where you can relax and recharge?

Designate a space in your home that is completely off-limits to ministry work, conversations, and counseling—your personal breathing room. This should be a place where you can fully disconnect, recharge, and be yourself.

Having a space where you can unwind is essential for maintaining balance and avoiding burnout. Whether it is a cozy reading nook, a hobby corner, or a spot to watch your favorite show, give yourself permission to step away from the demands of ministry. Rest is not a luxury; it is a necessity for longevity in both life and leadership.

Communication. Are there times when church members contact you or your husband outside of reasonable hours? Do you have a set time when you are unavailable for church matters?

Establishing set times when you and your husband are available—and times when you are not—is crucial. Ministry is demanding, but it should not consume every aspect of your life. Just as the church has designated service hours, you must also set boundaries to protect your time together. Outside of true emergencies, there should be moments in your day and week when you are simply unavailable.

I recall a time when this principle was put to the test. A few years ago, we were about to embark on a long-awaited vacation, preparing to set sail on our very first cruise. The day before our departure, a church member's mother transitioned to be with the Lord. She called to inform us, and while our hearts went out to her, we had already planned to be away for over a week. We expressed our deepest condolences and let her know we would not be returning immediately.

She ultimately decided to wait until our return to hold the service, but I wrestled with feelings of guilt for not being there in person to comfort the family. However, I had to remind myself that setting boundaries was not neglect—it was necessary. Had we canceled our plans every time a need arose, we would have never truly been able to rest. Ministry is a calling, but it does not mean sacrificing every personal moment. Establishing and honoring boundaries allows us to serve more effectively, without losing ourselves in the process.

Reflecting on these areas will help you identify where boundaries are needed to prevent overextension and protect your personal and family life.

Setting Clear Boundaries

Once you have identified the areas that need boundaries, the next step is to establish clear and specific limits. Healthy boundaries protect your marriage, well-being, and effectiveness in ministry. Here is how to implement them effectively:

Define your limits. Be intentional about what is acceptable and what is not. For instance, you might decide that weekday evenings after a certain hour are dedicated to family time or that you will only commit to a set number of church events per month. Clearly outlining these limits ensures that both you and your spouse prioritize your relationship without guilt or burnout.

Communicate boundaries clearly. Boundaries are only effective if clearly communicated. Share them openly with your spouse, family, and church members. Explain why they are necessary for maintaining balance and sustaining long-term ministry effectiveness. Use a kind yet firm approach, reinforcing that these limits enable you to serve better when you are rested and present.

Set consequences. Consistently enforce your boundaries so they are respected. If someone contacts you after your designated personal time, choose not to respond until the next day. If a request exceeds the limits you have set, politely decline. When others see that you are serious about maintaining these boundaries, they will learn to respect them.

By defining, communicating, and enforcing your boundaries, you create a healthier environment that allows both your marriage and ministry to thrive.

Overcoming Challenges in Maintaining Boundaries

Maintaining boundaries can be particularly challenging in ministry, where the needs of others often seem immediate and pressing. However, boundaries are essential for sustaining both your well-being and your ability to serve effectively. Here are some common challenges you may encounter—and ways to overcome them:

Guilt. Saying no or limiting your involvement can trigger feelings of guilt, especially when others expect you to always be available. Remember that prioritizing your well-being allows you to serve with greater energy and effectiveness in the long run. A depleted leader cannot pour into others. Taking care of yourself and your marriage is not selfish; it is necessary.

Pushback is inevitable. Not everyone will immediately understand or respect your boundaries. Some may question your decisions or attempt to guilt-trip you into changing them. Stay firm and consistent. Over time, people will adjust as they realize that your limits are non-negotiable and essential for maintaining a balanced life.

Flexibility. While upholding boundaries is crucial, there will be moments when exceptions are necessary, such as true emergencies or unique situations. However, be mindful that occasional flexibility does not become a pattern that erodes your boundaries. If flexibility becomes the norm, your limits will lose their effectiveness.

By acknowledging these challenges and preparing for them, you can maintain boundaries that support both your marriage and ministry, ensuring that you serve from a place of strength rather than exhaustion.

Reaping the Benefits of Healthy Boundaries

Establishing and maintaining healthy boundaries enables you to thrive both personally and in ministry. By prioritizing balance, you not only protect yourself but also enhance your relationships and effectiveness in serving others. The key benefits include:

Improved well-being. Boundaries safeguard your mental, emotional, and physical health by preventing burnout and reducing stress. When you create space for rest and self-care, you replenish your energy and are better equipped to handle the demands of ministry.

Stronger marriage. By dedicating intentional time and energy to your marriage, you reinforce your relationship, establishing a solid foundation for both your personal life and ministry. A healthy, connected marriage sets a powerful example for your congregation and offers the support you need to navigate ministry challenges together.

Effective ministry. When you are not overextended, you can serve with greater joy, clarity, and effectiveness. Boundaries allow you to be fully present in your ministry work without feeling drained or resentful, ultimately benefiting the entire church community.

Identifying and maintaining healthy boundaries is not a one-time decision but an ongoing process that evolves with your needs and circumstances. Regularly reassessing your boundaries and making necessary adjustments ensures that you continue to lead a balanced, fulfilling life—one where both your marriage and ministry can thrive.

Take Time for Self-Care

Prioritizing self-care is essential for maintaining balance in both marriage and ministry. When you take care of yourself, you show up more present, engaged, and effective in all aspects of your life.

Individual time. Ensure that both of you have space for personal hobbies, interests, or simple moments of relaxation. Whether it involves reading, exercising, crafting, or enjoying a favorite activity, this personal time helps recharge your energy and prevents burnout. A well-rested and fulfilled individual is better equipped to contribute to a strong marriage and effective ministry.

Physical health. Encourage each other to maintain a healthy lifestyle through regular exercise, balanced nutrition, and adequate rest. Physical well-being has a direct impact on emotional and spiritual health. When your body is cared for, your mind is clearer, your stress levels are lower, and your ability to serve with joy increases.

Seek support. Ministry life comes with unique challenges, and you do not have to navigate them alone. Look for guidance from counselors, mentors, or support groups that understand the demands of ministry. Having a safe space to process challenges and receive encouragement provides valuable perspective and strengthens your ability to handle the pressures of leadership.

Self-care is not selfish; it is necessary. When you prioritize your well-being, you not only benefit yourself but also enrich your marriage, ministry, and those you serve.

Regularly Review and Reflect

Maintaining a healthy balance between marriage and ministry is an ongoing process. As life and ministry evolve, it is important to regularly evaluate and adjust to ensure that both remain strong and fulfilling.

Review and reflect. Set aside time periodically to assess how well you are maintaining balance. Engage in open discussions about what is working and what needs to change. Are your boundaries being respected? Are both of you feeling fulfilled in your marriage and ministry? Reflection helps you remain proactive in addressing challenges before they become overwhelming.

Flexibility. While boundaries and routines are important, ministry life is unpredictable. Be willing to adjust your strategies as circumstances change. Whether accommodating a new church responsibility, navigating shifts in family dynamics, or pursuing personal growth, flexibility enables you to tackle new challenges while prioritizing your marriage.

Regular reflection and a willingness to adapt enable both your marriage and ministry to thrive in harmony, fostering a relationship built on mutual support, understanding, and shared purpose.

Reflection Questions

1. What are some signs that suggest you need to establish clearer boundaries between your ministry and personal life?
2. Have you clearly defined what is acceptable and what is not regarding ministry obligations?
3. How can you communicate your boundaries to your spouse, family, and church members?
4. What steps can you take to ensure that your boundaries are consistently respected?
5. Have you ever experienced guilt when enforcing your boundaries? How did you handle it?
6. How do you respond when others push back against the boundaries you have set?
7. In what ways can you maintain flexibility without compromising your boundaries?

Journal Your Thoughts

CHAPTER 4
Family Dynamics and Parenting

Meet Cynthia

Cynthia has been married to her pastor husband for 20 years. Early in their marriage, they dreamed of having a large family, but they postponed starting their family until later. Now, after two decades of marriage, they have three children: a 10-year-old daughter and 5-year-old twin boys. Her husband has pastored a mega church for over 20 years, and their children are being raised within that same church community.

Cynthia is deeply involved in the ministry. She plays a vital role in the Women's Ministry and helps establish a thriving Youth Department. Early in their marriage, she and her husband decided that she would be a stay-at-home mother until their daughter was older. However, when she became pregnant with twins, she chose to continue staying home to care for them.

Before having children, Cynthia was fully available for ministry. She assisted with outreach events, worked closely with the women's shelter, and supported her husband's pastoral duties. Once their children arrived, they were embraced by the congregation and received special attention. However, as time passed, Cynthia began to notice subtle yet troubling patterns in how her children were treated compared to others in the church.

The Pressure of Being the Pastor's Children

Cynthia's children were deeply loved by the congregation, but they were also held to a different standard.

The congregation showered them with special privileges; however, at the same time, they were judged more harshly than other children for normal childhood behavior.

One incident particularly stuck with Cynthia. One afternoon, during a church-sponsored outdoor family event, she overheard a group of older church mothers scolding her twin boys for being too rambunctious. "You are the pastor's children; you need to act like it," they told them.

Cynthia was furious. Her boys were not misbehaving; they were running and playing like all the other children. Why were her children expected to act differently? Why couldn't they be kids without the weight of their father's title dictating their behavior?

This frustration only deepened when she noticed a shift in her daughter's behavior. Her daughter, now ten, wanted more freedom—to participate in school activities with her friends and to enjoy experiences beyond the church. The church's expectations were weighing on her, and she began to resent the limitations imposed on her because of her father's role.

Tensions at home escalated. Cynthia's daughter began slamming doors, crying, and arguing with her mother. Then, one day, she uttered words that pierced Cynthia's heart:

"You care more about those people at church than you do about me. You never have time to spend with us."

Cynthia was devastated. Had she unknowingly prioritized ministry over motherhood? Was her dedication to the church coming at the cost of her relationship with her children?

The Conflict Between Family and Ministry

Cynthia, guilt-ridden and deeply shaken by her daughter's words, knew she needed to make a change. She sat down with her husband, hoping to discuss the issue and find a solution together.

While he listened patiently, his response was less than helpful. In his mind, he was called to ministry, and his family had been blessed by the privileges that came with his position. He believed their children were well-loved, well-provided for, and should be grateful for the life they had.

But Cynthia understood it was not that simple. She could see the emotional toll this was having on their children. She realized that their kids did not just need material things or the admiration of the congregation—they required time, attention, and a connection with their parents.

Determined to correct the imbalance, Cynthia made an intentional effort to spend more time with her children, engaging in their interests, listening to their concerns, and setting aside ministry obligations when necessary. For a while, things seemed to improve.

But the demands of the church were relentless. Slowly, Cynthia found herself falling back into the same patterns, the same cycle of putting the congregation's needs before her own family's needs.

And so, the struggle continued.

Cynthia's experience is not unique. Many pastors' wives struggle to find a balance between ministry, marriage, and motherhood. Here are some key lessons to learn from her story:

Children of pastors often face unfair expectations. Church members may unknowingly place unrealistic pressures on them, expecting them to be more mature, better behaved, or more spiritual than other children.

The ministry should never overshadow family. It is easy to get caught up in serving others, but children need time, love, and emotional connection with their parents just as much as the congregation does.

Pastors and their spouses need to be unified in their approach to parenting. A healthy discussion about balancing church and home life is crucial in ensuring both marriage and family thrive.

Healthy boundaries discussed in the previous chapter are also essential when raising children. Setting boundaries is crucial. Without clear boundaries, the demands of ministry can consume family time, leading to strained relationships and resentment.

Being intentional about quality time is important. It involves not only spending time together but also being fully present during that time.

Work-Life Integration: Scheduling Family Time Amid Weekend Services, Meetings, and Social Events

One of the biggest struggles for pastors' wives is finding the right balance between ministry commitments and family life. Unlike a traditional job, pastoral ministry is not confined to a 9-to-5 schedule; it extends into evenings, weekends, and holidays. Church services, counseling sessions, leadership meetings, and community events can easily consume time, leaving little room for spouses, children, and personal well-being.

While demand for availability is high, it is possible to integrate ministry and family life in a way that prioritizes both without sacrificing one for the other. Achieving this balance requires intentional scheduling, clear boundaries, and a willingness to say no when necessary.

The Challenge of Work-Life Balance in Ministry

Unlike most careers, pastoral work is deeply personal, and the lines between work and home can blur quickly. Here are some common challenges pastors' wives face:

Ministry commitments are unpredictable. A sudden hospital visit, crisis counseling, or a funeral can disrupt family plans.

Weekends are often consumed by church activities. Sundays are not days off, and Saturdays are frequently filled with weddings, rehearsals, or outreach events.

Evening meetings and events take priority. Midweek Bible studies, leadership meetings, and ministry gatherings can make family dinners a rarity.

Holidays and special occasions are shared. Christmas, Easter, and other celebrations are often spent with the church family instead of at home.

Technology makes it harder to disconnect, as texts, emails, and phone calls can interrupt family time at any moment.

Without intentional planning, these factors can strain marriages, cause children to feel neglected, and lead to burnout.

Strategies for Integrating Work and Family Life

Instead of fighting against the nature of ministry, you can take practical steps to blend work and family life in a way that benefits both.

Prioritize and Schedule Family Time Like a Non-Negotiable Commitment

Ministry will always demand your time, but your family needs to know they are just as important. One of the best ways to protect family time is to schedule it on the calendar, just as you would for a ministry meeting.

Set family appointments. Block out specific days or hours each week for uninterrupted family time. Treat these moments as sacred as a church event.

Weekly family nights. Whether it is game night, movie night, or a special dinner, create a predictable routine where your kids know they have your full attention.

Plan date nights. Your marriage should be nurtured, not just maintained. Set aside at least one evening a month for just you and your spouse.

Take a regular sabbath. Choose a consistent day to unplug from ministry and focus on rest and relationships.

Set Healthy Boundaries Between Ministry and Home Life

Boundaries are not selfish—they are essential for longevity in ministry. Without them, you will constantly feel pulled in different directions.

Limit after-hours calls and texts. Decide on set hours when you and your husband are off-duty, except for true emergencies.

Say no without guilt. Not every church request requires your immediate attention. If a meeting or event conflicts with family time, consider delegating it or rescheduling.

Be fully present. When you are with your family, be fully engaged—put the phone away, turn off email notifications, and resist multitasking.

Incorporate Your Family into Ministry (Without Forcing It)

Rather than compartmentalizing family and ministry, look for ways to integrate them naturally.

Make church a joyful experience for your kids. Avoid making them feel forced into activities, but encourage their participation in ways they enjoy.

Plan family-friendly ministry activities. Involve your kids in church events, community service, and enjoyable outings so that ministry feels inclusive rather than separate.

Consider taking ministry trips together. When possible, make conferences, retreats, or mission trips a family affair.

Encourage your husband to prioritize family moments. If your children see their father setting boundaries for the family, they will feel valued and secure.

Protect Special Occasions and Create Family Traditions

One of the biggest sacrifices in ministry is missing family celebrations due to church commitments. While some occasions are unavoidable, others can be protected with advance planning.

Celebrate holidays on different days. If your husband is busy on Christmas Eve or Easter Sunday, create your family traditions on a different day.

Plan family getaways in advance. Block off time each year for a family vacation or retreat, even if it is a short trip.

Make birthdays and anniversaries special. Even if you cannot celebrate on the exact date, prioritize quality time before or after.

Reflection Questions

1. In what ways have you, like Cynthia, felt torn between your ministry responsibilities and the needs of your children or family?
2. How do you handle the pressure of public expectations placed on your children because of your or your spouse's role in ministry?
3. Have you ever unintentionally prioritized church duties over your family's needs?
4. How do you and your spouse navigate differing perspectives on parenting within the demands of church leadership?
5. How can you create sacred, uninterrupted time with your children that assures them of your love and attention?
6. Have you ever witnessed or experienced unfair treatment of ministry children by others in the congregation?
7. What are two practical steps you can take this week to strengthen the emotional connection between you and your children?

Journal Your Thoughts

CHAPTER 5

The Challenge of Extended Family Expectations

Meet Cecilia

Cecilia and her husband had faithfully pastored their local church for many years. When her sister Donna's family relocated to the area, Cecilia was thrilled. Not only was she gaining the joy of having her sister nearby, but Donna was also a seasoned church member with strong leadership experience. Cecilia viewed her sister's move as a divine opportunity to enhance and support ministry efforts.

Initially, things appeared promising. Donna jumped right in, joining auxiliaries, volunteering, and offering help wherever she could. However, after a few months, Cecilia noticed subtle shifts: volunteer morale was dropping, participation was dwindling, and murmurs of discontent began to circulate.

What she discovered was disheartening.

Donna, though well-intentioned, had begun to dominate the ministries she joined. Other leaders felt overrun, voiceless, and disrespected. Worse, some shared that Donna was leveraging her relationship with Cecilia—implying she knew what was best because she was "the First Lady's sister."

Cecilia was crushed.

Caught between her loyalty to her sister and her calling to serve and protect the church body, she faced a painful dilemma. If she ignored it, morale might worsen. But confronting her sister could damage their relationship.

With grace and prayerful resolve, Cecilia chose to lead with honesty and humility. She arranged a meeting with Donna and the auxiliary leaders. The atmosphere was tense at first, but once hearts were opened, healing began. Donna realized that her good intentions had been miscommunicated through an overbearing approach. The ministry leaders acknowledged their hesitancy to speak up due to Donna's familial tie to Cecilia.

The breakthrough did not come through confrontation—it came through conversation.

Many pastors' wives experience family pressure in different ways.

In-laws with strong opinions on church leadership. Some in-laws, especially those from a long line of ministers, may have firm beliefs about how a pastor's wife should serve. You may hear comments like, "Your role is to stand beside your husband at all times," or "You should be leading women's ministry"—even if that is not where you feel called.

Relatives want special treatment. Family members may assume they are entitled to special privileges in the church simply because they are related to the pastor. They may assume they should receive preferred seating, leadership roles, financial assistance, or influence in decision-making. Navigating these expectations without causing family strife can be challenging.

Pressure to prioritize family over church commitments. On the other hand, some family members may not understand the demands of ministry. You may hear things like, "You are always at the church—what about your family?" or "You missed the family reunion again because of church?" These comments can stir up guilt and make you question whether you divide your time fairly.

Cultural or traditional expectations. In some cultures, there are strong gender roles or family hierarchies that dictate how a pastor's wife should behave. Family elders may expect submission, public reserve, or specific church involvement, even if it does not align with your personal strengths or calling.

Navigating These Expectations with Wisdom

Instead of feeling trapped by extended family expectations, you can set healthy boundaries (here it is again) while still honoring and respecting them. Here is how:

Establish clear boundaries with your spouse. Before addressing family expectations, you and your husband must be on the same page. Discuss your roles in the church and at home, and agree on boundaries regarding family involvement, leadership roles, and time commitments.

Ask. What do *we* want our ministry and marriage to look like?

Decide. How much influence will the extended family have in church matters?

Agree. How will we handle family members' requests for special treatment?

Maintaining a unified stance can help prevent family conflicts from causing division between you and your husband.

Communicate firmly yet respectfully. When extended family members offer unsolicited advice or try to impose expectations, respond with grace and firmness.

If your in-laws insist that you should be involved in a specific ministry, you can say, "I truly appreciate your thoughts. Right now, I am serving where I feel led, but I am always open to new opportunities as God guides me."

If family members expect special privileges, kindly remind them, "We love having you as part of our church family, and we treat all members equally, regardless of personal relationships."

If relatives pressure you to prioritize family over ministry, reassure them, "I deeply value family time, and I am working hard to balance both. Let's plan ahead for special moments together."

Your tone matters; staying kind yet firm helps set boundaries without alienating loved ones.

Prioritize family without guilt. Your first ministry is your home. If you feel guilty or conflicted about spending time away from extended family due to ministry, consider:

Scheduling family time intentionally is essential. Plan regular family visits, vacations, or virtual check-ins so relatives do not feel neglected.

Delegating church responsibilities. If you are overcommitted, delegate tasks in ministry to free up more family time.

Letting go of guilt. You cannot please everyone. Prioritize what truly matters and release the burden of meeting every expectation.

Recognize when to step back. If family tensions become too overwhelming, it may be necessary to create distance for your emotional well-being.

Limit discussions about church leadership decisions with relatives.

Seek wise counsel from a trusted mentor or a pastor's wife who has navigated similar situations.

Pray for wisdom on handling difficult family relationships without resentment.

Reflection Questions

1. Have you ever experienced a situation where a family member became involved in your ministry?

2. Do you believe your experience with the family member had a healthy outcome?

3. How did Cecilia's story resonate with your own experience?

4. What boundaries currently exist between your family and your role in ministry?

5. Have you and your husband had clear conversations about how family members should be involved in the church?

6. In what areas might you need to better define or enforce boundaries with extended family?

7. Think of a time when you had to respond firmly yet respectfully to a family member. What did you learn from that experience?

Journal Your Thoughts

CHAPTER 6

Spiritual Life and Self-Care

Meet Lauren

Lauren has been a pastor's wife for five years. As she sat in the back pew after the last service of the day, clutching her lukewarm cup of coffee, the church was nearly empty—only a few volunteers tidying up. Yet her mind buzzed with the swirl of ministry details. She had greeted countless church members that morning, volunteered in the children's ministry, and helped organize a luncheon for visiting missionaries. Outwardly, Lauren appeared calm and composed, the quintessential pastor's wife. Inwardly, though, she felt drained, her spiritual reservoir running on fumes.

Her Bible lay open beside her, yet she realized she had not read a single verse that day. She moved from one task to another, offering prayers for others without pausing to pray for herself. A subtle guilt gnawed at her, whispering that she should be the most spiritually grounded person in the building—after all, she was "the pastor's wife." Yet here she was, exhausted and discouraged, wondering when her relationship with God had turned into a series of obligations rather than a source of life. As she sipped her coffee, the questions weighed heavily: How could she guide others in their faith when her own felt so depleted? And where could she go to reconnect with God on a personal level?

This chapter explores why prioritizing your spiritual well-being and self-care is essential, as well as how to maintain it despite the many responsibilities vying for your attention.

As a pastor's wife, you must cultivate a vibrant faith to sustain you through the various demands of ministry. A pastor's wife should prioritize her relationship with God over the routine tasks expected by the congregation.

Church life can inadvertently turn faith into a series of tasks, sermons, Bible studies, and event planning. While these are good endeavors, they can overshadow the fact that Christianity is fundamentally a relationship with Christ. Set aside time each day for personal devotion—whether it is an early-morning prayer walk, a midday Scripture reading, or journaling at night. Allow God to speak to you in the stillness, not just through structured programs.

Take the time to recognize the signs of routine-driven faith.

We Focus on Checklists Instead of Connection

When daily devotions become mere tasks, it is time to pause. You might be reading Scripture or saying prayers, but if your heart is not engaged, you risk missing God's voice in those moments. We find ourselves checking boxes because we know these are the daily responsibilities we need to address. We perform these actions without much thought or feeling, making them feel like a "job." It reaches a point where, if we forget, we criticize ourselves and struggle with feelings of guilt.

Resentment Over Responsibilities

Feeling annoyed or burdened by the very activities meant to nurture your faith, such as attending midweek worship or leading a women's group, can signal that you are stuck in a routine. Resentment can creep in without your realizing it. It may start with looking at your calendar and feeling overwhelmed by the schedule. Then, you find yourself making excuses not to participate and feeling guilty about these emotions. But the truth is that you are so tired and do not know how to express what you feel.

Lack of Personal Joy

If you find yourself talking about God more than talking to Him, or serving others without being personally refreshed, your faith has likely become mechanical rather than relational. The energy required to always be available to counsel others, pray for them, and walk them through one crisis after another can lead to spiritual burnout.

Take the Time to Rediscover the Heart Behind Spiritual Practices

Embrace the "Why." There are times when you will ask yourself, "Why am I doing this again?" Why am I spending all my time with intercessory prayer sessions, Bible study, and worship? When we engage in spiritual practices—prayer, Bible study, and worship—it is easy to slip into autopilot.

We may attend prayer meetings, read a set amount of Scripture, or sing along during worship without truly reflecting on why we are engaging in these activities in the first place. Recapturing your motivation for each spiritual practice can renew your passion, deepen your faith, and shift your focus from mere duty to genuine devotion. When you remember why you are doing them (to experience His presence and guidance), these practices regain their meaning.

Focus on Intimacy, Not Performance

Instead of setting a quota for how many chapters of the Bible you read, aim for heartfelt interaction with God. Linger on a verse that resonates with you, journal a response, or sit quietly, allowing Him to speak to your soul.

The Importance of Self-Care

In our scenario with Lauren, we see that she failed to prioritize her self-care. She was experiencing burnout, feeling distressed and depressed, despite doing what she felt called to do. Self-care is more than a short getaway, a lunch date with girlfriends, or a spa day. Self-care is the intentional practice of nurturing your mind, body, spirit, and emotions.

It is not about indulgence or selfishness—it is about stewarding the vessel that God has entrusted to you. In ministry, especially as a pastor's wife, you constantly pour out, offering your time, energy, empathy, wisdom, and presence. If you are not careful, you may give from an empty cup, which can lead to exhaustion, resentment, or burnout.

True self-care honors God because it acknowledges your human limitations and your need for replenishment, allowing you to serve from a place of overflow rather than depletion.

Why Self-Care Matters for Pastors' Wives

As a pastor's wife, you often carry the weight of high expectations, many of which are unspoken or internalized. You may feel pressured to always be available, attend every event, and meet everyone's needs, sometimes at the expense of your well-being.

But here is the truth: you are not the Savior—Jesus is. Your role is to serve faithfully, not endlessly.

Self-care affirms your worth apart from your roles and responsibilities.

Self-care protects your joy and helps prevent bitterness toward ministry.

Self-care strengthens your witness by modeling healthy boundaries and God-honoring stewardship of life. The four pillars of self-care are:

Physical Self-Care

"Or do you not know that your body is a temple of the Holy Spirit within you…?" – 1 Corinthians 6:19

Rest. Prioritize sleep and Sabbath rest. A tired body cannot function at its best, spiritually or emotionally.

Nutrition. Fuel your body with healthy food. What you eat affects your energy, mood, and focus.

Movement. Regular exercise, even a short walk, relieves stress and boosts your physical and emotional resilience.

Medical Care. Keep up with your check-ups. Do not ignore pain or health issues because you are "too busy."

Emotional Self-Care

"Above all else, guard your heart, for everything you do flows from it." – Proverbs 4:23

Know your limits. Learn to say "no" when needed. Overcommitting can lead to resentment and burnout.

Express yourself. Journaling, counseling, or talking to a trusted friend helps release built-up emotions.

Do what brings joy. Engage in hobbies or activities that make you feel alive—reading, baking, gardening, painting. These are not distractions; they are life-giving.

Spiritual Self-Care

"Come to Me, all who are weary and burdened, and I will give you rest." – Matthew 11:28

Quiet time. Protect your personal time with God. Ministry work is not a substitute for intimacy with Him.

Worship and prayer. Take time to praise God, not just in service planning, but in solitude and sincerity.

Fellowship for you. Find a small group, prayer partner, or pastors' wives support group where you are being poured into, not just leading.

Mental Self-Care

Mental rest. Unplug from social media and church texts at times to clear your mind.

Continual learning. Read books or listen to podcasts that feed your soul, expand your understanding, and inspire you.

Healthy thought life. Practice renewing your mind with truth (Romans 12:2). Replace self-criticism with grace-filled affirmations.

Common Barriers to Self-Care in Ministry Life

- "If I rest, I will let someone down."
- "Other people have it worse—who am I to need a break?"
- "My worth is tied to how much I serve."
- "I feel guilty when I take time for myself."

These thoughts are lies dressed up as humility. The enemy would love to keep you overworked and overwhelmed because a depleted servant is a discouraged servant. Jesus Himself often withdrew to rest and pray. If he needed it, so do you.

How to Begin Practicing Self-Care

Start small. Dedicate 15 minutes a day just for yourself. No ministry discussions, no multitasking - just something life-giving.

Block out time weekly. Schedule moments of rest, fun, and replenishment just as you would schedule church events.

Communicate your needs. Discuss with your spouse and ministry team how to protect your time without guilt or apology.

Give yourself permission. You are allowed to rest, be tired, and take a break.

Self-care is not selfish. It is stewardship. When you care for yourself, you are not stepping away from your calling— you are honoring it. You acknowledge that you are human, created by a loving God who never asked you to carry the weight of ministry alone.

You are most powerful in ministry not when you are constantly busy, but when you are spiritually rooted, emotionally whole, physically rested, and mentally clear. Give yourself the care you so willingly extend to others— your marriage, your church, and your calling will flourish as a result.

Reflection Questions

1. Can you relate to Lauren's experience of spiritual depletion?
2. In what ways has your relationship with God become more routine than relational?
3. Do you find yourself serving others while neglecting your spiritual nourishment?
4. What does your current devotional life look like?
5. Have you felt guilty for needing rest, space, or personal time apart from ministry responsibilities?
6. Which of the "routine-driven faith" signs—checklists, resentment, lack of joy—have you experienced recently?
7. When was the last time you did something simply because it brought you joy, not because it was productive?

Journal Your Thoughts

CHAPTER 7

Church Relationships and Community

Meet Martha

Martha was a newlywed, deeply in love with her husband, who served as the pastor of a vibrant local church. After their wedding, she moved to his city, leaving behind her family, friends, and familiar routines. As she adjusted to her new life, she began attending church regularly, volunteering, and participating in events, but something was missing. She was surrounded by people, yet deeply lonely.

With no real community outside the church, Martha craved genuine friendships, someone to talk to, laugh with, and share life's ups and downs. That is when she met Jill, a long-time church member who seemed warm, welcoming, and full of energy. Over time, their bond grew. They went shopping together, grabbed lunch after service, and attended local events. Jill became Martha's closest friend—and her confidant.

Feeling safe with Jill, Martha slowly let her guard down. She began to share more deeply: her feelings of isolation, her struggles adjusting to her husband's demanding schedule, and even some of the disappointments she felt in their marriage. What she did not realize was that Jill's loyalty was not as strong as she had assumed.

One day, out of the blue, Martha's husband approached her, frustrated, hurt, and confused. He had just spoken with Jill, who had shared many of the personal and private things

Martha had confided in her. Not only that, but Jill had begun speaking with other women in the church as well.

Martha was stunned. Her heart sank as she realized what had happened: the person she trusted most outside her marriage had taken her vulnerability and turned it into gossip. She was not just embarrassed; she was heartbroken. She had opened her heart in search of friendship and found betrayal instead.

As a pastor's wife, you live in the delicate space between leadership and relationship. You are expected to connect with people, support the ministry, and be "approachable"—yet also manage your life and heart with discretion. It is not always easy. You may long for genuine friendships but also feel unsure about how transparent you can be. While you may love the people you serve, you can still feel lonely in the crowd.

This chapter is about finding your place in the ministry without losing your peace, your boundaries, or your authentic self.

Fostering genuine friendships. Church life is full of warm smiles, kind greetings, and surface-level conversations. However, behind those smiles, many pastors' wives quietly crave something deeper—real, trustworthy friendships. Relationships where you can laugh freely, pray honestly, and show up without performing. Friendships where you are not just "the pastor's wife" but are known and valued as a woman.

However, if we are honest, forming these kinds of connections in ministry is not always easy. Being in a leadership role means maintaining a delicate balance: close enough to connect but wise enough to guard your heart. Openness can feel risky, especially when the lines between personal and pastoral become blurred.

So, how do you build authentic relationships in a space that can feel guarded or conditional?

Start with discernment. Not everyone needs access to your private world, and that is okay. You do not have to open your whole heart to everyone you meet. Ask God for discernment. Pray for eyes to see who is emotionally safe, spiritually mature, and trustworthy. Allow relationships to unfold naturally over time. Discernment is not the same as distrust; it is wisdom.

Look for consistency, character, and spiritual fruit. Safe people may not be the loudest or most visible; they often listen more than they talk and handle others' stories with care.

Be approachable, not exposed. There is a difference between authenticity and oversharing. Being real does not mean revealing every detail of your life to everyone. It means showing up with honesty, warmth, and humility—without feeling the need to perform or pretend.

You can be kind without being naive. You can be friendly without being overly familiar. You can be open without being wide open. Protecting your heart does not mean shutting it off. It means knowing who to entrust it to.

Pursue mutual connection. True friendship is not one-sided. Look for relationships with mutual care, respect, and emotional investment, not just people who want access to your time, advice, or influence through your husband.

The healthiest friendships are those in which both individuals feel free to be vulnerable, where encouragement flows in both directions, and where your presence is valued, not just your position.

Sometimes these friendships may come from within your church; others may be found outside of it. That is okay. What matters most is the quality, not the proximity.

"A friend loves at all times, and a brother is born for a time of adversity." – Proverbs 17:17

This kind of love—steady, dependable, and grace-filled— is worth praying for, watching for, and waiting for.

One of the most challenging aspects of ministry is the reality that, no matter how kind or sincere you are, someone will misunderstand you. You will be misquoted, misjudged, and occasionally misrepresented. As a pastor's wife, you often live under a magnifying glass, where your outfit, smile (or lack thereof), social media posts, and even your level of involvement in church events are all scrutinized and sometimes critiqued.

And when people do not speak directly to you but instead talk about you, that is even harder. So, how do you handle it when you find out someone has said something unkind, inaccurate, or just plain unfair?

Do not take it personally—Even when it feels personal. Criticism in ministry can sting because it often strikes at the very core of who you are and what you value most: your family, your faith, and your service to God. Yet, most criticism says more about the speaker than the target. People project disappointments, frustrations, and unmet expectations onto visible leaders—especially pastors' wives—because they represent spiritual authority and emotional safety all at once.

When an unkind comment lands on your doorstep, remind yourself:

Context matters. Consider what might be happening in this person's life that prompted such words.

Identity matters more. Ground yourself in the unchanging truth that you are fully known, loved, and approved by God, regardless of human opinions.

Perspective brings peace. Criticism is fleeting; Christ's affirmation is eternal.

"Am I now trying to win the approval of men, or of God? ... If I were still trying to please people, I would not be a servant of Christ." – Galatians 1:10

Your value was sealed at the cross, not in the comment section, the church foyer, or the latest social media thread. When you anchor your worth in Christ, criticism loses its power to define you.

Respond with truth, not retaliation. Jesus never shrank from speaking truth—yet He did so with gentleness, courage, and love. When rumors or harsh words threaten unity, the goal is not to silence critics but to elevate the conversation.

You do not have to defend yourself to everyone. Sometimes, silence, anchored in prayerful confidence, speaks volumes.

You do not need to respond to every comment. Engage only when prompted by the Spirit, not provoked by ego.

Step in when harm is spreading. If misinformation damages someone's reputation or fractures relationships, address it calmly, clearly, and privately whenever possible.

Practical steps:

1. Pause and pray before replying—ask the Holy Spirit for tone, timing, and words.
2. Clarify, do not condemn—state the facts without attacking motives.
3. Invite reconciliation—offer a way forward, such as a face-to-face conversation, shared prayer, or mutual apology.

"Instead, speaking the truth in love, we will grow to become in every respect the mature body of Him who is the head, that is, Christ." – Ephesians 4:15

Grace-soaked truth, delivered with steady composure, lets your character—and Christ's character—speak louder than any rumor ever could.

Encouraging a Culture of Connection

As a pastor's wife, you have a unique opportunity to set the tone for a warm and inclusive church family. Everyone longs for a sense of belonging; we are created in God's image for relationship, not isolation. In fact, being part of a church community is essential for both spiritual growth and emotional well-being. By actively nurturing connections through small, sincere gestures of love, you can help your congregation feel more like a supportive family than just Sunday acquaintances. Even simple acts, such as a smile or a greeting, can ripple out and uplift someone's spirit. Scripture likens the church to a body in which each member is needed (1 Cor. 12:12); when people feel connected and valued, the whole body thrives. The following are key ways you can encourage a culture of connection in your church through warm leadership, intentional relationships, and community-building actions.

Lead by Example

Church members often take cues from the pastor and his wife. When you consistently model genuine care and friendliness, others feel inspired to do the same. The Apostle Paul's instruction to young Timothy could apply to you as well: "set the believers an example in speech, in conduct, in love, in faith, in purity." In practical terms, this means being the first to reach out and welcome others, showing humility and kindness in all your interactions. For instance, make it a point to arrive a bit early to services so you can greet people at the door with a warm smile and a handshake. Do not underestimate this – "smiling goes a long way" in making others feel at ease. If you are open and approachable, people will sense it.

Leading by example also involves authenticity. Church members need to see that you are a real person with joys and struggles, just like them. One pastor's wife discovered that being "real" and admitting personal struggles helped other women feel more comfortable around her. It gave them permission to be 'real' too. You set the tone when you show that it is okay to ask for prayer or admit a challenge. This wise transparency, while still maintaining appropriate discretion, demonstrates humility and builds trust. Others will follow suit, creating a community where people can truly know and support each other rather than feel pressured to pretend everything is perfect.

Practical ways to lead by example in building connections:

Initiate conversations. Do not wait for others to approach you; walk up, say hello, and learn names. Taking the initiative to connect with others can break the ice. For example, if you see someone new or alone at coffee hour, go introduce yourself and ask a few questions to get to know them.

Listen actively. Warm leadership involves more than just talking. Encourage others to share by asking genuine questions about their week or their family, and listen attentively. Your interest helps people feel valued. As James 1:19 reminds us, *"be quick to listen, slow to speak."* Active listening shows love.

Participate and serve alongside others by joining in church events, small groups, or service projects rather than staying on the sidelines. If there is a clean-up day, roll up your sleeves with everyone else. By joyfully serving, you demonstrate that no task is beneath you and that everyone's contributions matter. Jesus Himself washed His disciples' feet as an example of servant-leadership (John 13:14-15).

Model a positive attitude. Your calm, hopeful demeanor in stressful moments can reassure the church. For instance, if a Sunday school program is chaotic, your patience and humor can diffuse tension and show others how to respond with grace. *"Not domineering... but being examples to the flock"* is how Scripture describes godly leaders.

When you lead in these ways, you subtly influence the overall atmosphere. Over time, a culture of friendliness and unity will take root as people reflect the example you have set. Your genuine warmth can help newcomers and longtime members alike feel, "This is a place I belong."

Celebrate Others

One beautiful way to foster connection is by celebrating the people around you. In a healthy church family, everyone should feel seen and appreciated. As Romans 12:10 urges, *"Love one another with brotherly affection."* Outdo one another in showing honor. When you make it your mission to honor and encourage others, you create an uplifting environment where belonging thrives. A pastor's wife can profoundly shape the culture through how she talks about and acknowledges people's contributions and joys.

Start by noticing the little things that others do and thank them sincerely. Did someone arrange the flowers on the altar or help clean up after the fellowship lunch? Thank them, either privately with a note or publicly if appropriate. Genuine appreciation makes people feel valued and motivates them to stay connected. The Bible says, *"Therefore, encourage one another and build one another up." (1 Thess. 5:11)*

Simple words of affirmation can go a long way in building someone up. For example, tell the children's ministry volunteer, "I so appreciate how you make the kids feel loved each week," or commend the youth who ran the tech booth, "Great job today – you really helped the service run smoothly!" Such comments may seem small to you, but they can deeply encourage someone's heart.

Celebrating others also means rejoicing in their joys and weeping in their sorrows (Romans 12:15). Make it a habit to highlight milestones and victories in people's lives. If a member has a new baby, a graduation, or even a smaller victory like overcoming an illness, acknowledge it and rejoice with them. You could organize a brief shout-out during announcements or in the church newsletter: "Let's congratulate Maria on finishing her degree!" This shows people that their church family cares about their life events. Likewise, be quick to comfort those who are hurting or grieving—a simple "We're standing with you" demonstrates that they are not alone.

Another aspect of this is deflecting praise to others. As a pastor's wife, you might often receive thanks for church events or ministries. Use those moments to highlight others who contributed: "Oh, our team did an amazing job – Sue and Alice put so much love into this dinner." This humility not only honors those individuals but also teaches the entire church to value each member's role.

The Bible compares the church to a body, where every part is needed, "the parts that seem weaker are indispensable" (1 Cor. 12:22) and deserve honor. When you celebrate the quieter contributors and "outdo yourself in honoring" them, you send a powerful message: everyone matters here.

Consider the example of Barnabas in the New Testament. His name literally means "son of encouragement," and he lived up to it by constantly supporting and affirming others. He vouched for Paul when others were wary (Acts 9:26-27), and he encouraged John Mark to the point of restoration (Acts 15:37-39). Inspired by Barnabas, you can become a daughter of encouragement in your church.

Be the one who notices growth in a shy member and says, "I see how you stepped out of your comfort zone – that's awesome." Or celebrate a faithful prayer warrior by acknowledging their behind-the-scenes ministry. When people feel celebrated rather than overlooked, their sense of belonging deepens, and the church becomes a more joyful, united community.

Practical Ways to Celebrate and Encourage Others

Personal thank-you notes or messages. Write a quick text or handwritten note to at least one person each week, thanking them for something specific you have observed. For example: "Julie, the way you welcomed those new visitors on Sunday was such a blessing. Thank you for serving with such a warm heart!" This personal touch can brighten someone's day.

Spotlight others' contributions. If your church has a bulletin, newsletter, or social media page, consider adding a "volunteer spotlight" or "member appreciation" segment. Highlight a different person periodically—share a bit about what they do and express gratitude for them. This not only honors that person but also helps the congregation appreciate each other more.

Celebrate life events. Keep a calendar of birthdays, anniversaries, or significant events of church members. You might send a card or have the church sing Happy Birthday. It does not have to be elaborate; even mentioning it in conversation shows you care. "Rejoice with those who rejoice" by sharing in their happy moments.

Encourage both publicly and privately. In group settings, do not hesitate to praise and thank others by name, while being sensitive to those who prefer to remain quiet. One-on-one, offer encouraging feedback, such as, "I notice how faithfully you attend the prayer group; you inspire me." Both public affirmation and private encouragement foster a culture where people feel appreciated.

By consistently celebrating others, you will help your church to become a place where honor and gratitude flow freely. Instead of feeling taken for granted, people will know their church family is cheering them on. This practice knits hearts together and reflects the love of Christ, "who did not come to be served, but to serve" (Mark 10:45). In an atmosphere of mutual encouragement, emotional and spiritual health can flourish.

Model Hospitality

Few things break down barriers and draw people into the community like genuine hospitality. When you open your heart and home to others, you demonstrate Christ-like love in action. The Bible urges believers to be hospitable, as seen in the verse, *"Offer hospitality to one another without grumbling"* (1 Peter 4:9). As a pastor's wife, you can set the pace by making hospitality a hallmark of your ministry. This does not require a picture-perfect home or a lavish meal; it is about making people feel welcome and "at home" in your presence. Even small gestures of hospitality can help strangers become friends and make the church feel like a true family.

Begin with simple steps right at church. For example, be intentional about seeking out newcomers after the service and chatting with them. Introduce them to others with shared interests to help them make connections. You might say, "Have you met Tom? He is also a teacher like you," to spark a conversation. If someone you meet is new to the area or does not know many people, consider inviting them to join you for lunch or coffee soon. It can be as easy as saying, "A few of us usually grab coffee after church; we would love for you to come along!" Such invitations extend fellowship beyond the church walls and allow relationships to grow.

When possible, use your home as a ministry tool. In the early church, believers "broke bread in their homes and ate together with glad and sincere hearts," and the result was an increase in unity and joy. You might host a small group Bible study in your living room, a casual game night, or a potluck dinner. Do not worry about having everything perfect; your warmth matters more than your furniture or cooking skills. A plate of cookies and a listening ear can minister more deeply than an elaborate dinner served with stress. One pastor's wife recalls how nervous she was the first time she hosted the youth group, but her simple effort of hosting a taco night turned into laughter, bonding, and even impromptu worship with guitars. The teens later said her home felt like a safe haven. That is the power of hospitality – it opens hearts.

Modeling hospitality also means encouraging others in the church to practice it. As you host and welcome, you can gently inspire others to do the same. Perhaps you could organize church-wide opportunities for connection, such as monthly after-service potlucks or "dinner for eight" rotations, where people mix and share meals at each other's homes.

Lead the way by helping to coordinate and participate. When people see you prioritizing fellowship, they will understand that building community is a value, not an afterthought. Hebrews 13:2 reminds us, *"Do not neglect to show hospitality to strangers, for by so doing some have entertained angels without knowing it."* When you warmly welcome newcomers or church "strangers," you never know what blessings you might be ushering in – you could be encouraging a future leader or simply being Jesus's hands and feet to someone in need.

Practical ways to model hospitality. Invite people into your home in small ways. You do not need to plan a fancy dinner party. Start with inviting one or two individuals or a family over after church for a simple lunch or dessert. Keep it informal – the goal is relaxed fellowship. You could say, "We usually heat pizza or make sandwiches after church; would you like to join us this Sunday?" The casual invitation can mean a lot to someone who usually eats alone.

Start a hospitality routine at church. For instance, create a "coffee and cookies" corner after services where visitors can meet the church leaders. You could bring a tray of treats and personally introduce newcomers to others in that space. Your efforts to foster a welcoming environment at church set a hospitable tone.

Encourage a buddy system by pairing longtime members with newer attendees for informal dinners. You might quietly ask a friendly family in the church, "Would you be willing to have our new couple over for dinner sometime? I think you would enjoy getting to know them." By mobilizing others to host, you enhance the spirit of hospitality.

Be inclusive in invitations. When planning social gatherings, such as holiday parties and outings, consider those who might feel left out and include them. As the pastor's wife, your invitation carries weight. If you invite the single older gentleman to the church picnic and save him a seat at your table, others will notice and hopefully follow your example next time. Look for the lonely or those on the fringes and draw them in.

In practicing hospitality, you embody Christ's welcome. Your kindness in action, whether through a cup of tea in your kitchen or a warm hug in the sanctuary, creates an environment where people feel they belong. Over time, these gestures weave individuals into a community that laughs, prays, and walks through life together. A church that "opens its doors" and hearts widely will be rich in fellowship and love.

Small Gestures, Big Impact

Never doubt that the little things you do out of love can have a big impact. In fact, it is often the small, day-to-day gestures that touch hearts most deeply. One church member noted that "the smallest expressions of interest and kindness can have a significant impact. Many people come to church carrying unseen burdens, feeling lonely or invisible in the crowd. A simple hello or a kind word from you might be exactly what they need to feel noticed by God and by others. No act of kindness is too small in the Lord's service. Jesus said even giving a cup of water to someone in His name matters in God's eyes: *"Anyone who gives you a cup of water in my name because you belong to Christ will certainly not lose his reward."* In the same way, your small acts of care are seen by God and can profoundly encourage a person.

Consider the small opportunities that present themselves each week. Is there a shy teenager hanging out at the back of the sanctuary? Walk up and ask how school is going. Is an elderly widow sitting alone? Sit beside her during the service or ask if she would like to share lunch. These little actions can change someone's entire day.

One pastor's wife shared that there was a couple in her church who intentionally sat in the back pew so they could greet latecomers or infrequent attendees with a hug and a warm welcome. That simple practice made those "barely there" folks feel seen and loved, and often it encouraged them to keep coming back. Another couple deliberately sat in a different section of the church each week to meet new people. These are small adjustments with huge relational payoffs—they noticed people who might otherwise slip through the cracks.

Think of remembering names – a small gesture that tells someone, "You matter enough for me to remember you." If you greet a newcomer by name on their second visit, you might see their face light up with appreciation. Similarly, a quick phone call or text to someone who missed a Sunday saying, "Hey, we missed you today, hope everything's okay," can make them feel incredibly cared for. Little acts, like baking cookies for a family going through a hard time or saving a seat for a new mom struggling with her kids, speak love louder than we imagine. They communicate, "You belong, and we've got you."

The beauty of small gestures lies in the fact that anyone can perform them, and they create a ripple effect of kindness. When you consistently practice these micro-connecting actions, others in the church will catch on, and your warmth will be contagious. A culture of connection develops not only during big events or programs but also in these everyday moments of reaching out. Galatians 6:2 says, *"Bear one another's burdens, and so fulfill the law of Christ."* Often, we help bear burdens through small kindnesses – a listening ear here, a helping hand there. Over time, these little seeds of love grow into a widespread sense of caring throughout the church.

Ideas for Small but Impactful Gestures

Greeting with genuine warmth. Make eye contact, smile, and say a heartfelt hello to people, both familiar faces and new ones. Use their name if you know it. Feeling truly greeted and seen when one walks into church can set a positive tone for their whole worship experience.

Noticing the "quiet" people. Pay attention to those who may hover on the sidelines: the introvert, the teen, the person who slips in late. A quick check-in, such as "How are you doing? I am glad you are here," can validate their presence. If someone frequently sits alone, occasionally sitting with them or inviting them to join your row can make a difference.

Offer a prayer on the spot. If someone mentions they are struggling or feeling anxious about something, do not just promise to pray later—if appropriate, take a moment right then and there. A 30-second prayer in the lobby ("Lord, please give my sister peace this week...") can profoundly comfort someone and make them feel supported.

Little tokens of care. Keep an eye out for small ways to brighten someone's day. It might involve giving a flower from the bouquet to a first-time visitor, handing a $5 coffee gift card to a tired single mom, or bringing soup to a sick member. These gestures, though small, echo God's love. Remember, even one kind word or touch can be a ministry.

In God's economy, small seeds of kindness can yield a great harvest. Your gentle touch on one person's life may encourage them to reach out to another. By faithfully doing the "small stuff," you help weave a tapestry of compassion in your church where each person feels they belong and are cared for. It is often through these humble, quiet acts that the Holy Spirit works to bind hearts together.

Fostering a Sense of Belonging for Emotional and Spiritual Health

Cultivating a culture of connection is not merely a nice extra; it is essential to the emotional and spiritual health of your congregation. When people experience genuine belonging in the church, it provides a foundation of support that enables them to thrive. Modern studies confirm what Scripture has long taught: involvement in a caring faith community can reduce loneliness, stress, and even depression. In a connected church, individuals understand they do not have to carry life's burdens alone. They have friends to pray with during crises, mentors to encourage their spiritual growth, and a family in Christ to celebrate joys and navigate sorrows. This type of fellowship serves as a safety net for our hearts. "Two are better than one... if either falls, one can help the other up" (Ecclesiastes 4:9-10).

Spiritually, a sense of belonging draws us closer to Christ. We grow best when we grow together. Hebrews 10:24-25 highlights the importance of believers meeting together to encourage one another, *"stirring up one another to love and good works."* In a warm church community, individuals are more likely to engage in Bible studies, serve using their gifts, and persevere in faith because they feel supported by and accountable to a loving community.

James 5:16 even tells us to confess our sins to one another and pray for one another, implying a level of trust and connection that only emerges in an atmosphere of grace. By fostering that atmosphere, you create a safe space for spiritual healing and growth. Those who might hesitate to be open in a colder environment will find the freedom to seek help, ask questions, and draw nearer to Jesus when they know they are among caring friends.

Emotionally, belonging to a church family combats the isolation that many individuals in our world feel. Loneliness can be crippling, but the church is God's antidote – *"God sets the lonely in families"* (Psalm 68:6). Your efforts to connect people ensure that the widow has daughters and sons in Christ checking on her, the struggling teenager has adoptive aunts and uncles in the faith to guide him, and the young parents have seasoned couples to turn to for advice. Over time, these bonds significantly improve people's resilience and mental health. One Christian counselor noted that for believers, "being part of a church family is essential to both spiritual and emotional health." We truly are holistic beings – when our hearts are supported, our spirits soar, and vice versa.

By fostering a culture of connection, you facilitate the kind of fellowship described in the New Testament, a place where people are accepted, loved, and supported. In such an environment, individuals can experience the love of Christ in tangible ways through the care of others. This not only fortifies their emotional well-being but also reflects the Gospel to those who witness the love in action. Jesus said, *"By this everyone will know that you are my disciples, if you love one another"* (John 13:35). In a church marked by genuine connection and love, even outsiders will notice that something is different—they will see Christ's love at work.

Be encouraged that every warm greeting, every shared meal, and every note of encouragement you offer is a ministry of love that strengthens Christ's body. In God's eyes, your hospitality and kindness are not forgotten; they build up His church. When you help create a community where people feel they belong, you are tending to souls and honoring the Lord's command to love. Sometimes the fruit of your efforts will be visible quickly, as when a newcomer blossoms into a committed member because they felt welcomed. Other times, you may not see the full impact, but trust that *"Your labor in the Lord is not in vain"* (1 Cor. 15:58). You are planting seeds of connection that can yield eternal fruit.

As a pastor's wife, you set the tone through your caring actions. Your warm leadership can transform a group of Sunday attendees into a genuine church family. Continue leading by example, demonstrating Christ's character in your interactions. Keep celebrating others to ensure each person feels valued. Practice hospitality in both big and small ways, opening doors for friendship. And remember, small gestures done in love have a profound impact – they are like loaves and fishes that Jesus can multiply. By doing these things, you reflect the love of Jesus, the Good Shepherd who knows each of His sheep by name.

In the end, fostering a culture of connection is about reflecting God's heart. God *"first loved us"* (1 John 4:19), and through your caring actions, others will feel a touch of that divine love. A connected, caring church not only enriches emotional and spiritual health within its walls but also becomes a beacon of hope to the surrounding community. Your role in this is invaluable. With each person who feels seen and each heart that feels safe, you contribute to a healthier, holier church where Christ's love reigns. So, keep sowing those seeds of connection—God is using you to nurture a beautiful harvest of faith and fellowship in your church.

Reflection Questions

1. Can you identify with Martha's desire for friendship and her hurt from betrayal?
2. What boundaries do you currently have in place around personal sharing and relationships within the church?
3. When discerning who to trust, what qualities do you look for in a friend?
4. How do you typically respond to criticism or gossip within the church?
5. When did you last celebrate or affirm someone in your church community?
6. How are you modeling hospitality in your personal life and ministry?
7. What is one step you could take this month to open your heart or home in a way that reflects Christ's love?

Journal Your Thoughts

CHAPTER 8

Effective Ministry Leadership

Meet Karen

Karen was thrilled to work in the ministry alongside her husband, who pastored a small country church. She loved the warm congregation, the heartfelt worship, and the peaceful atmosphere that surrounded their ministry. Although she did not hold a formal leadership role, she faithfully supported her husband and was content to serve behind the scenes.

One day, her husband asked if she would consider taking on a more prominent leadership position. The church's women's ministry needed guidance, and he believed she would be an excellent fit. Excited and honored, Karen embraced the challenge with enthusiasm and eagerness to serve the women of the church. However, it was not long before reality set in.

Though the group had functioned for years without a designated leader, the transition was not as smooth as she had hoped. Some of the women welcomed her warmly, while others were hesitant, questioning her authority and scrutinizing her decisions. Karen, who entered the role with sincere intentions, found herself caught off guard by the undercurrent of resistance.

She began to second-guess herself. At times, she wondered if she was trying too hard and doing too much; other times, she worried that she was not doing enough. When she finally shared her frustrations with her husband, he gently explained, "The women have led themselves for a long time. It will take time for them to trust your leadership."

One of the most discouraging patterns emerged when any suggestion Karen made was followed by someone quietly checking with her husband. "Did she really say that?" "Is that what you want us to do?" This constant need for confirmation undermined her confidence and authority. Frustrated, Karen told her husband, "You need to stop allowing them to bypass me like this—or I will step down."

He agreed to support her publicly but reminded her of an important truth: "You have been asked to lead, not just fill a position. That means earning their trust, not borrowing mine."

That conversation shifted everything.

Karen realized she had been trying to lead based on how she thought the women expected her to lead or how her husband would lead. But what they needed most was not a carbon copy of someone else; they needed her—her heart, her vision, and her unique leadership style. She did not need to prove herself; she needed to embrace who God had already equipped her to be.

Leadership is a part of your divine assignment—whether you embrace a visible role or lead quietly behind the scenes. As a pastor's wife, people naturally look to you for guidance, example, and encouragement. Even if you did not sign up to lead, your position places you in a space of influence. The question is not whether you are a leader; it is how you will lead. This chapter will help you do so with grace, confidence, and clarity.

Embracing Leadership Roles: Accepting the Call to Lead

For many pastors' wives, the idea of stepping into leadership brings hesitation. It is not always a fear of the role itself, but rather a fear of the judgment, criticism, or burden that leadership seems to carry. Some worry that they are not qualified. Others feel unworthy because their gifts do not fit the traditional mold of ministry leadership. But here is the truth: God does not call the perfect—He calls the willing.

Leadership in ministry is not about being flawless or knowing all the answers. It is about walking in obedience, leading with humility, and having a heart that is ready to serve. It is not about filling someone else's shoes or replicating your husband's leadership style; it is about faithfully showing up as your true self.

You do not have to lead everything. Perhaps you are not called to the pulpit, and that is perfectly okay. You might thrive in one-on-one discipleship, behind-the-scenes planning, coordinating care teams, or simply being a quiet source of wisdom for other women. Leadership comes in many forms—find your path and walk it with confidence.

Start where you are. Leadership begins with small steps. It may involve opening your home for Bible study, checking in on a struggling mother in your congregation, or stepping in to organize community outreach. These acts of faithfulness have a profound impact. You do not have to "arrive" to be used by God—you must be available.

"Whoever wants to become great among you must be your servant." – Matthew 20:26

That Scripture serves as a reminder that greatness in God's kingdom is measured not by titles or applause, but by the posture of your heart. When you lead from a place of service, you reflect the heart of Christ, and that is where true leadership begins.

Leading with Confidence and Grace

You do not have to lead like anyone else—just lead like you, covered in grace, guided by the Spirit, and rooted in the truth of who God says you are. Confidence is not pride—it is faith in action. And grace is not weakness—it is power made perfect in humility.

Once you have accepted the call to lead, the next step is to lead with confidence and grace, not with arrogance or self-reliance, but with the quiet, unwavering assurance that God has called you, equipped you, and is walking with you every step of the way.

As a pastor's wife, your leadership presence may be public, subtle, or somewhere in between. Regardless of how visible your role is, your influence is real, and people are watching. The way you carry yourself can give others permission to walk in freedom, serve with joy, and lead authentically. Here is how to do it effectively:

Lead from Your Strengths. God did not design you to be a carbon copy of someone else. Your leadership does not have to mirror that of your husband, your predecessor, or the most admired woman in your denomination. You are uniquely shaped by your experiences, personality, spiritual gifts, and passions for a purpose.

Are you a great listener? Use it to connect deeply with the women in your congregation.

Are you well-organized? Assist in streamlining ministry events and structures.

Do you have a heart for encouragement? Use words, notes, or prayers to uplift others.

Whatever your strengths are, embrace them. Operating within your God-given abilities brings ease and impact. You will lead more naturally, and your authenticity will create space for others to shine in their gifts as well.

Model Servant Leadership

True leadership is not about titles, applause, or being in control; it is about service. Jesus, the greatest leader of all, knelt and washed the feet of his followers. He loved unconditionally, met people in their mess, and never demanded status or recognition.

- Be approachable. Let people see the real you, not a performance, but a person.
- Be consistent. Participate in the small things, not just the spotlight moments.
- Be gracious. Show the same patience, love, and flexibility that you require from others.
- When you lead with humility and compassion, people are drawn not just to your leadership, but to the Jesus they see in you.

Guard Your Heart

Leadership comes with both honor and scrutiny. There will be moments when you are misunderstood, overlooked, or criticized. It is in those moments that you must anchor your identity not in applause or outcomes, but in Christ alone.

"Am I now trying to win the approval of men, or of God? Or am I trying to please men? If I were still trying to please men, I would not be a servant of Christ." – Galatians 1:10

Do not let the fear of people's opinions keep you from moving forward. And do not let praise make you forget where your strength comes from. Keep your heart soft before God and let Him shape how you respond to praise and pressure.

- Build regular time into your schedule to reconnect with God, outside of your leadership responsibilities.
- Surround yourself with those who speak the truth and provide encouragement, rather than mere flattery.
- Remember that your worth does not change based on your performance—it is secured by grace.

Developing Others: Mentoring New Leaders

One of the most impactful roles you will ever play in ministry is not necessarily behind a pulpit—it is across the table from another woman who is just getting started. As a pastor's wife, you carry not only influence but insight. And when you intentionally pour wisdom into others, you help shape the next generation of leaders in your church and beyond.

Mentorship does not require a formal program or perfect timing; it simply begins with a willing heart.

Be accessible. You do not need a title or an agenda to make a difference. Sometimes, the most meaningful mentorship occurs over coffee, during a phone call, or while folding bulletins together. Invite someone into your world. Ask questions, listen, and pray with them.

Share your story. You do not have to have it all figured out—just be honest. Your struggles, stumbles, and victories will speak volumes to someone walking a similar path. Transparency builds trust.

Lead by example. Whether you realize it or not, someone is always watching. The way you serve, speak, and handle challenges serves as a model for others. Your calm during conflict, your grace under pressure, and your steady devotion to God all provide quiet yet powerful lessons.

Mentoring is less about providing all the answers and more about being present, authentic, and available. It involves walking alongside someone and reminding them, "You do not have to do this alone."

Nurturing Future Pastors' Wives

Few people truly understand the unique weight of being a pastor's wife—except for another pastor's wife. When you meet a young woman stepping into this role, your encouragement and support can be life-giving.

Many new or soon-to-be pastors' wives often feel uncertain, overwhelmed, or isolated. They may struggle to reconcile their identities with the expectations placed upon them. You have the opportunity to provide wisdom and grace as they navigate this unfamiliar territory.

Normalize the struggle. Let them know it is okay to feel conflicted, overwhelmed, or out of place. Everyone has a learning curve, and struggling does not disqualify them; it prepares them.

Provide practical wisdom. Offer tips on setting healthy boundaries, developing consistent prayer habits, managing time effectively, and knowing when to say "no." Practical help builds confidence.

Encourage their individuality. Remind them that they do not have to fit a certain mold. God called them for a reason, and He will use their unique personalities, backgrounds, and gifts to serve the church in their authentic way.

Sometimes, your simple assurance, "You are not alone, and you are enough," can make all the difference.

Creating a Healthy Leadership Culture

A healthy church is not built by one person doing everything; it is built by many people, empowered to lead with excellence and humility. As a leader, you help set the tone for how others serve, relate, and grow. That is why it is important to be intentional about creating a culture where others are trusted, celebrated, and supported.

Empower others; avoid micromanagement. Resist the urge to control every detail. Instead, trust others with responsibility, even if they approach tasks differently from you. Growth occurs when people feel trusted, not watched.

Celebrate contributions. Take the time to recognize and affirm the efforts of those around you. A simple thank-you, a shoutout in a meeting, or a handwritten note can go a long way in building morale and momentum.

Model humility. Be the kind of leader who admits mistakes, apologizes when necessary, and remains teachable. Humility disarms tension and builds lasting respect. People follow leaders who are real, not untouchable.

When you foster a culture of empowerment, grace, and mutual respect, leadership becomes a joy rather than a burden. You create an atmosphere where people flourish, and ministry thrives.

Resolving Conflicts: Addressing Tension Head-On

Where there are people, there will be problems. It is not a lack of faith; it is a fact of life. Even in the church, where we strive to walk in love and unity, misunderstandings occur. Personalities clash, expectations are missed, and emotions run high. And yes, conflict arises in ministry as well.

As a pastor's wife, you may witness disagreements among team members, tension within leadership, or passive-aggressive behavior in planning meetings. You may even be pulled into conflict directly or asked to mediate when others are at odds.

Avoiding conflict may seem like the safest route, but avoidance does not bring peace. It only delays resolution and often deepens division. Healthy leadership means learning to confront issues with grace, courage, and a heart for restoration.

Be Proactive, Not Passive

Letting issues fester only increases frustration. What starts as a simple misunderstanding can grow into resentment or bitterness if left unchecked. Addressing tension early is key.

Pray before you speak, but do not put off the conversation indefinitely. Ask God for wisdom and the right timing.

Use clear, kind communication. Speak from your heart, not from a place of hurt.

Do not wait until you reach your breaking point. Approach others with love, not out of frustration or exhaustion.

"If your brother or sister sins, go and point out their fault, just between the two of you." – Matthew 18:15

This principle applies not only to sin issues but also serves as a blueprint for healthy communication. Private, prayerful confrontation prevents public fallout.

Listen to Understand

Effective conflict resolution begins with listening rather than responding. Many conflicts persist simply because people feel unheard or misunderstood.

Let each person speak without interruption. Resist the urge to defend yourself or correct them mid-sentence.

Ask clarifying questions to ensure you fully understand their perspective.

Even if you disagree, validate their feelings. Saying, "I can see why that upset you," does not mean you are admitting fault; it shows empathy.

When people feel seen and heard, their posture softens. Understanding builds bridges where defenses once stood.

Speak the Truth in Love

Honesty and grace must go hand in hand. Confronting issues does not mean being harsh or confrontational; it means being truthful with kindness.

Be clear but not critical. Use "I" statements rather than accusations. ("I felt hurt when…" instead of "You always…")

Avoid sarcasm, shaming, or spiritual manipulation. Words are powerful; use them to heal, not wound.

Do not merely vent your emotions—offer a path forward. A spirit of reconciliation is more important than being "right."

"Instead, speaking the truth in love, we will grow to become in every respect the mature body of him who is the head, that is, Christ." – Ephesians 4:15

Growth comes through truth, but truth spoken in love.

Tools for Mediation

Sometimes, as a pastor's wife, you may find yourself in the midst of disagreements among church members, ministry leaders, or even volunteers. While it is not your responsibility to resolve every issue, you may be called upon to help create a space for reconciliation. This is where mediation, conducted with grace and intention, can make a significant difference.

Here are a few tools to help facilitate healthy, God-honoring dialogue:

Choose a neutral setting. The environment matters. Avoid addressing heated issues in high-traffic areas like the church foyer or immediately after a service. Instead, schedule a time to meet in a private, calm space where everyone can feel safe and heard. Creating emotional and physical space for peace encourages more productive conversation.

Establish ground rules. Before the conversation begins, set expectations. Remind all parties to:

- Speak respectfully.
- Avoid interrupting.
- Stay focused on the current issue (do not dredge up the past unless it is relevant to healing).
- Use "I" statements rather than accusations. Ground rules help ensure the conversation is constructive, not destructive.

Focus on reconciliation, not victory. The goal is not to determine who is right—it is to restore unity. Encourage each person to seek understanding rather than dominance. Ask, "What would healing look like for both of you?" Center the conversation on grace, not grudges.

"Blessed are the peacemakers, for they will be called children of God." – Matthew 5:9

Your role is not to fix the problem but to create space for healing. And that is a beautiful act of ministry.

Knowing When to Involve Others

There will be times when a conflict exceeds your emotional or spiritual capacity to mediate, and that is okay. You were never meant to carry every burden alone.

Know your limits. If a situation continues to escalate, becomes toxic, or involves sensitive issues such as accusations or legal concerns, it is time to involve a trusted church elder, counselor, or trained mediator. Escalating responsibly is not a failure; it is wisdom.

Protect your spouse's perspective. It may be tempting to share every detail of church conflicts with your husband, especially since he is the pastor. However, discretion is crucial. He is already shouldering the weight of leadership. Whenever possible, manage minor tensions discreetly to avoid unintentionally burdening or biasing him before he needs to be involved.

"Plans fail for lack of counsel, but with many advisers they succeed." – Proverbs 15:22

Healthy leadership understands when to stand firm and when to seek assistance. There is no weakness in seeking guidance; it demonstrates strength and spiritual maturity.

Reflection Questions

1. Can you relate to Karen's experience of stepping into leadership with excitement, only to meet resistance or doubt?
2. Have you ever felt pressure to lead like someone else—your husband, a former leader, or a peer?
3. What are some of the leadership strengths God has uniquely given you?
4. When has servant leadership been most difficult for you to model?
5. What does it look like for you to lead with both grace and humility in those moments?
6. How do you guard your heart from both criticism and praise?
7. What practices help you stay rooted in God's approval rather than public opinion?

Journal Your Thoughts

CHAPTER 9

Perseverance Through Trials

Meet Lisa

Lisa had been a pastor's wife for over a decade. She was devoted to her church, loved her husband, and poured herself into the ministry with all her heart. From women's conferences to youth retreats, hospitality, counseling, and running the children's department, Lisa wore many hats—and she wore them well. However, life hit hard.

It began with a health scare. What she thought was merely fatigue turned into a full diagnosis—an autoimmune disorder that drained her strength and left her in pain. Doctor visits became routine, and some days, simply getting out of bed felt like a victory.

At the same time, the church entered a period of transition. Its congregation had merged with another church, and Lisa watched as long-time members quietly slipped away. The new culture brought new expectations—and not all of them were kind. Rumors began to swirl. Lisa's role was questioned. Some said she was pulling away; others thought she was controlling. Neither was true. She was trying to survive.

Then came the spiritual attacks. At night, she would lie in bed and hear a whisper in her heart: "You are not enough. You are failing him. You are failing them. Maybe you were never called to this." She did not know how to fight back. She was too tired to pray, too weary to talk, and too embarrassed to admit that she was burned out.

One Sunday morning, as she sat in the back of the sanctuary, tears welled up in her eyes while the worship team sang, "You are my strength when I am weak." For the first time in months, she felt God's presence envelop her like a warm blanket.

That moment did not resolve everything; however, it marked a turning point.

Lisa began to step back—not from the calling, but from the chaos. She started going to counseling. She let go of the need to be everywhere for everyone. She reached out to a few trusted friends and told them the truth: "I'm not okay, and I need help." To her surprise, they did not reject her; they rallied around her.

Through prayer, rest, and intentional support, Lisa found her way back—not to the version of herself who could do it all, but to the woman God had always loved—even in her weakness.

She says now, "That season broke me open—but it also rooted me deeper. I learned that I did not have to be the strong one all the time. I just had to be willing to be held."

Major Life Transitions

Lisa's story is not unique. Many pastors' wives encounter moments when life changes abruptly—when illness strikes, finances falter, or their entire church undergoes transformation. These are the moments when the ground beneath your feet shifts, and suddenly the rhythm of ministry that you once managed with grace feels heavy and unfamiliar.

Perhaps you have been there. Or perhaps you are experiencing it now.

- A child receives a difficult diagnosis.
- Your spouse's health or mental wellness begins to suffer.
- A job loss or unexpected expenses threaten your family's stability.
- The church you helped nurture through seasons of growth is now facing division, a relocation, or a leadership transition.

In these moments, ministry does not pause. The sermons keep coming. The members still have needs. You may feel guilty for not being "strong enough" to keep it all going.

However, the truth is that your humanity is not a disqualification; it is a divine reminder of your need for grace.

God never called you to carry every burden. He called you to abide in Him. This means it is okay to slow down, step back, and ask for help. It is okay to grieve what you have lost or what you fear losing.

"We are hard pressed on every side, but not crushed; perplexed, but not in despair; persecuted, but not abandoned; struck down, but not destroyed." – 2 Corinthians 4:8-9

Life transitions are not a sign of failure. They are invitations to trust God more deeply and lean into the support He provides—through prayer, through people, and through rest.

Spiritual Warfare

Not all battles in ministry are visible. Some do not arise from meetings, headlines, or clear explanations. Some battles occur quietly—in the unseen spaces of the heart and spirit. They manifest as waves of discouragement, subtle lies, sleepless nights, and emotional fatigue that feels deeper than burnout.

These are the signs of spiritual warfare.

As a pastor's wife, you are not just a support to your husband; you are a spiritual force in your own right. Your prayers, your presence, your obedience—they matter, and they are recognized by heaven and hell.

- That is why the enemy works hard to wear you down.
- He will whisper that your prayers are not effective.
- He will create division in relationships that once felt safe.
- He will promote isolation so you do not feel like you can reach out.
- He will use exhaustion to silence your spiritual authority.

At times, spiritual warfare manifests as church drama. At other times, it appears as self-doubt, depression, or a sudden loss of peace. However, beneath it all lies a very real enemy who seeks to distract, discourage, and disconnect you from your power source—God.

So, how do you fight back?

Pray with Power

You do not need fancy words; just honest ones. Declare God's truth even when your emotions do not align. Speak life into your home. Pray over your husband, your children, your mind, and your rest.

"The effectual fervent prayer of a righteous woman availeth much." – James 5:16 (paraphrased)

When you feel too tired to pray lengthy prayers, opt for shorter, more focused ones. Call upon the name of Jesus, whisper scripture, or play worship music and allow it to fill your atmosphere.

Fast with Intention

Fasting is a spiritual discipline that clears the clutter and heightens our sensitivity to God. When you fast—whether from something simple like social media or sugar—you create space to hear and move with God again.

Some breakthroughs only emerge when we press deeper. Do not be afraid to fast for clarity, strength, or healing during a battle season.

Invite Support

You are not meant to fight alone.

Find your "Aaron and Hur"—the people who will hold up your arms when you are too tired to stand. Whether it is a prayer partner, a small group, or a trusted friend, let someone know when you are struggling. There is no shame in saying, "Can you pray for me? I feel under attack."

"Though one may be overpowered, two can defend themselves. A cord of three strands is not quickly broken." – Ecclesiastes 4:12

There is power in agreement. There is covering in community.

Refueling Your Calling

Burnout does not always begin with a loud crash. Sometimes, it sneaks in through slow depletion—a hundred little yeses you thought you could handle. The late nights. The constant giving. The invisible emotional labor. And before you realize it, the fire that once burned so brightly for ministry feels more like smoke.

If you have ever thought, "I cannot keep doing this," you are not alone.

Many pastors' wives hit this wall and silently wonder if it means they have failed. However, burnout does not mean you are broken; it means you need to pause and refill.

It means your spirit is saying what your calendar will not admit: "I need rest. I need joy. I need to remember why I am doing this."

So, how do you refuel your calling?

Remember Your Why

Before the titles, the roles, and the routines, remember the moment you said yes to this life. Revisit the calling that stirred your spirit. What did God speak to your heart at that time? What dreams did you carry?

Revisit your journals. Look at old photos from your early ministry days. Reconnect with the passion that has been buried under obligation.

"Restore to me the joy of your salvation and uphold me with a willing spirit." – Psalm 51:12

Joy is not a luxury—it is a lifeline.

Prioritize Rest Without Guilt

Even Jesus stepped away to rest. You are not exempt. Rest is not laziness; it is a form of obedience.

Take a day off. Say no without providing an explanation. Protect your mental, spiritual, and emotional bandwidth.

A well-rested version of you is far more impactful than an exhausted you pretending to be fine.

Rediscover What Fills You

What makes you laugh again? What restores your sense of wonder? For some, it is reading. For others, it is creating, walking, painting, or simply sitting still.

Ministry does not have to smother your joy. Find what revives you and give yourself permission to engage with it again.

Recalibrate Your Rhythms

Maybe what once worked no longer fits. Seasons change, kids grow, and churches evolve. It is okay to realign your commitments.

Build new rhythms that include soul care:

- Quiet time in the morning

- Journaling or devotionals
- A counseling or mentorship check-in
- Unplugged family time

You were never meant to serve from an empty well. Refueling does not make you selfish; it makes you sustainable.

Reflection Questions

1. Have you ever experienced a season like Lisa's—physically, emotionally, or spiritually overwhelming?
2. What unexpected transitions or challenges have shaken your sense of balance in life or ministry?
3. When facing life-altering situations (illness, loss, financial crisis, etc.), how easy or difficult is it for you to ask for help?
4. Who is part of your support system, and who might you need to reach out to?
5. What lies or doubts has the enemy tried to plant in your heart during hard seasons?
6. What are some subtle signs of spiritual warfare you have noticed in your life or relationships?
7. Who are your "Aaron and Hur," the ones who can help hold your arms up when you are weary?

Journal Your Thoughts

EPILOGUE

Still Standing, Still Serving

A Life of Grace and Grit

You have walked through the pages of this book, met women like Cynthia, Sally, Camilla, Martha, Cecilia, Taneka, Lauren, Karen, and Lisa—each with a different story, yet all holding the same sacred tension: the divine call and the human heart. Maybe you saw pieces of yourself in their joys, their exhaustion, their growth, or their tears.

Being a pastor's wife is no small assignment. It is a calling filled with paradox: visibility and isolation, honor and heartbreak, influence and invisibility. You love deeply, lead quietly, and serve faithfully—all while juggling marriage, ministry, family, friendships, and your own identity.

This book was never meant to provide you with a polished formula—it was written to offer you grace for your journey. It serves as a reminder that you are not alone; God sees you, strengthens you, and sustains you—even when no one else fully understands the weight you carry.

Let's look back on what you have discovered:

Chapter 1: Identity in the Calling

You began by exploring the foundation, who you are beyond the title. We unpacked the unrealistic expectations, insecurities, and the need to reclaim your unique identity in Christ. You are more than "the pastor's wife," you are a woman called, loved, and chosen.

Chapter 2: Spiritual Life and Growth

We learned that spiritual strength does not come from performance but from personal intimacy with God. In the whirlwind of ministry, relationships must triumph over routine. Your soul matters, your rest matters, and your time with the Father fuels everything else.

Chapter 3: Balancing Marriage and Ministry

You can serve the church without sacrificing your marriage. We explored how to protect your connection with your spouse, establish boundaries, and prioritize each other, not just as leaders, but as lovers and friends. Your marriage is your first ministry.

Chapter 4: Family Dynamics and Parenting

Amid busy Sundays and midweek meetings, your children need more than a church program, they need their mother's presence and love. We discussed grace-filled parenting, flexibility, and how to give your children a healthy experience of ministry life.

Chapter 5: The Challenge of Extended Family Expectations

Extended family members serving within your ministry need not be a source of conflict; they can be a tremendous asset. While navigating family dynamics may present its share of challenges, it does not have to lead to division. Through honest conversation rather than confrontation, relationships can be strengthened, boundaries can be respected, and your ministry can flourish with the support of those you love. When guided by wisdom, prayer, and humility, family involvement can become a blessing rather than a burden.

Chapter 6: Spiritual Life and Self-Care

You are not a machine; you are a vessel—fragile yet filled with divine purpose. When you honor your need for rest, renewal, and emotional care, you lead from a place of abundance rather than depletion. Self-care is not selfish; it is stewardship.

Chapter 7: Church Relationships and Community

Ministry is deeply relational; however, it can often be a source of profound wounds. We have learned how to cultivate genuine friendships with discernment, respond to criticism with grace, and establish a culture of kindness and connection that starts with you.

Chapter 8: Effective Ministry Leadership

Whether you lead from the platform or the prayer closet, you are a leader. Your influence shapes the culture of your church. By leading with humility, mentoring others, and resolving conflicts wisely, you empower the next generation and reflect Christ's love.

Chapter 9: Perseverance Through Trials

Finally, we confronted the reality of suffering. When life collapses and the weight of the calling becomes overwhelming, you are still held. You are not disqualified by weakness; rather, you are deepened by it. In the valley, your roots grow stronger. Through spiritual warfare, burnout, and grief, your story becomes richer, more honest, and more beautiful.

Your Divine Assignment Continues

Dear sister in ministry, this is not the end of your story. It is simply the continuation of a life that makes an eternal impact, often in quiet, unseen ways. The phone call you answered, the meal you delivered, the smile you gave, the prayer you whispered—all of it matters to God.

You do not have to do it all. You do not need to have it all together. You must stay connected to the One who called you. He did not ask you to carry the weight of the world; He invited you to walk with Him.

So, take a breath. Re-center your heart. Lift your eyes.

You are still standing, still serving, still chosen.

And by God's grace, you will continue to survive—and thrive—through this divine assignment.

"Being confident of this, that He who began a good work in you will carry it on to completion until the day of Christ Jesus." – Philippians 1:6

Journal Your Thoughts

ABOUT THE AUTHOR

Overseer Salonge Crenshaw serves as the pastor of Union Outreach Fellowship Church in Farmville, Virginia, alongside her husband, Bishop Lylton C. Crenshaw. A devoted mother, grandmother, and teacher, she has impacted countless lives through preaching, counseling, and women's empowerment. Licensed to preach in 1997, her ministry began long before, marked by a powerful anointing to equip, heal, and set the captives free.

With a deep passion for holiness, purpose, and deliverance, Overseer Crenshaw embodies the spirit of Isaiah 40:31, *"They that wait upon the Lord shall renew their strength."*

She resides in Cartersville, VA, and continues to walk boldly in her divine assignment.

TO CONNECT

Follow us on Facebook @salongeCrenshaw

Visit Us to Learn More at: www.salongec.com, and

https://www.amazon.com/author/salongecrenshaw

www.ingramcontent.com/pod-product-compliance
Lightning Source LLC
Chambersburg PA
CBHW051528120626
46551CB00012B/1131

* 9 7 9 8 9 9 4 3 0 3 0 2 3 *